CREATIVE WORSHIP in Youth Ministry

BY DENNIS C. BENSON

Loveland, Colorado

Creative Worship in Youth Ministry

Copyright © 1985 by Dennis C. Benson

Third printing

Edited by Lee Sparks
Designed by Jean Bruns
Cover illustration by Judy Atwood
Illustrations by Craig Van Wechel

Library of Congress Cataloging-in-Publication Data

Benson, Dennis C.
  Creative worship in youth ministry.

  1. Young people's meetings (Church work)   2. Public worship.
3. Worship programs.   I. Title. BV29.B39   1985
264'.088055   85-24735   ISBN 0-931529-05-0

Printed in the United States of America

Foreword

The most important hour of the week! That's what the Sunday service *can* and *must* be if the church is to be the transformed, inspired and directed people of God. In the same way, moments of worship *can* and *must* be the most important times in the lives of church youth—times which shape the rest of their existence.

The subject of **Creative Worship in Youth Ministry** is large and very, very significant. We, as church leaders, have been self-indulgent and even foolish about the planning and designing of worship. We have gone on with worship services as usual, despite signs of boredom among young and old alike; we have dismissed many of the more adventurous new ways of worship; we have bolstered each other's prejudices in some churches as other churches have grown around us with their exuberant, participatory, energetic gatherings; we have shaken our heads at the eccentric patterns of the "youth culture" with its rock, strange fashions and mass gatherings, without learning what those movements represent in the lives of those young people.

Dennis Benson presents a challenging witness in **Creative Worship in Youth Ministry**. How blessed we are that Dennis has dedicated his time and enormous talents to the subject of youth worship. God has given many and diverse gifts to all of us; to Mr. Benson, God has given amazing gifts of imagination and creative energy. Throughout this book, Dennis' gifts stimulate our minds and enrich our experience. Our own expectations and work will never be the same again after we read his biblical commentaries, his presentations of needs and possibilities, and his marvelous examples of authentic and bold ways of worship.

Dennis Benson has made a career of listening for the Holy Spirit's breezes and watching for the flashes of God's light in the workings of human imagination and experience. Dennis especially has watched and listened for what God is doing among the youth of the world. He is perhaps the greatest listener and watcher among American church leaders today. Dennis has already led many thousands of contemporary Christians to deeper sharing and understanding of worship. We are grateful for the inspiration of **Creative Worship in Youth Ministry.** Although this resource contains many ideas for youth worship, much of what is written here could bring rich blessings to *all* ages.

Although we, as church leaders, have been easy on ourselves and have settled for the "traditional" and "usual" worship styles, many assessments and changes in Christian worship have occurred in recent years. For example, new translations of the Bible, new missals and prayer books, new songs, different kinds of vestments, colorful attention to the church year, new ways of participation such as physical action, etc. One reason that churches don't incorporate change into their worship services is because new ideas are often quite unsettling. Dennis Benson aids people as they respond to change by soothing unsettled feelings with his characteristic devotion to scripture, his respect for roots and traditions, and his beautiful sensitivity to people's feelings and needs.

But most of all, Dennis Benson serves us with his powers of imagination and his overflowing, creative love of young people and the whole family of God. Such powers and love are surely signs of the Spirit. Let them move us to new, conscientious efforts, so that worship by young people may become as important as stewardship programs, debates about social issues and reorganization of church structures.

Richard Avery and Donald Marsh
Proclamation Productions

Contents

CHAPTER 1

Introduction

The young man slowly sways back and forth in the pew. His body is damp with perspiration and his eyes blaze with excitement. The power in the room strikes him at many different levels. The sound (a blend of musical notes and human voices) runs a chill down his spine. He feels "goose" bumps on his arms. A sudden clarity sweeps his mind. Yes! Yes, it is now so obvious and possible! The God of all life is *his* God. The sinful aspects of the young man's personal life seem to fall aside. They are insignificant and meaningless: "I give my life to Jesus."

Such a scene has unfolded millions of times across the centuries. Men and women in every culture, in every possible kind of worship setting, and as part of every Christian tradition have found or been found by Jesus Christ. Worship has been a primary setting for the Spirit of God to change lives. Unfortunately, such mountaintop experiences are not always the usual component of today's worship services. There are many contemporary Christians, young and old, who have rarely experienced worship events that challenge, change, claim and comfort. Why?

I heard the slight sound of carefully placed footsteps above my head. I turned my head and glimpsed a disturbing sight. Four members of our youth group had slipped into the balcony of the sanctuary—at the end of the service!

I caught Bill, Dick, Duke and Tom before they could sneak away after the service. What had they been doing during the time of worship? The quartet confessed that they had been eating doughnuts at the coffee shop across the street. Why had they followed this pattern of missing worship? "It's boring; there's really nothing there for us."

The quartet was flawed in their thinking about church worship. It is the responsibility of each Christian to praise and glorify God regularly in public acts of worship. There is more to worship than being entertained, filling one's own needs and feeling good. A part of being a mature Christian is faithful participation with God's people. However, the young (and old) deserve worship opportunities in which they are included as participants with the company of all God's people.

My doughnut-loving quartet was expressing what I found later to be a common complaint in the church. "We want to encounter God in creative new ways. We are weary of out-of-date expressions of worship. We want to worship the God of today." That's when I began to explore new ways to worship the eternal God. And I found out that thousands of other Christians were searching along the same path. This book is the result of our experiences with creative worship in youth ministry.

A PLACE TO STAND

Before we plunge into a lively world of creative ideas for worship, we first must acknowledge our foundation. God is the sole authority of authentic worship. Our commitment to Jesus Christ prepares us for this unique relationship with our creator and sustainer. All glory and majesty belong to the only focus of our worship: God.

After the mountaintop experiences of the giving of the Law (Deuteronomy 6), the people were told to love the Lord God with all of their being. At every point in life, it is the task of the believer to teach the young this great goodness. This act of love is worship. There is a common temptation to separate the ritual of worship (service) and acts of worship (life). But such a division between the two realms is not biblically supported. The relationship between life and corporate worship is inseparably interwoven in the New Testament. Discipleship is inseparable from worship. The temple of God is everywhere. In wholistic worship, Christians integrate their rituals with their lifestyles.

The Bible provides a model for a total approach to worship in the familiar story of Moses and the burning bush (Exodus 3:1-10). This important encounter of calling, adoration and commission details God's initiation of the act of worship. The burning bush is the ultimate call to worship. The bush burns but is not destroyed. God chooses to use the human senses to beckon his servant. Moses can *feel* the heat and *see* the flames of the foliage which is not consumed. Moses decides to respond by seeking to understand what God is about and what God wants him to do.

When God sees that Moses has accepted this invitation, God speaks to him out of the bush. What would have happened if Moses hadn't pursued God's beckoning? God now calls Moses by name. The call to worship is personal. The dialogue continues. The servant is told that the common ground of the shepherd's path has been transformed into holy ground.

God tells the story of how Moses' forebears knew the Lord through his mighty acts. Moses is awed by this closeness with God. This worship scene transforms a common place into a setting of holiness and mystery.

At the very center of this worship experience, God lifts up the needs of his people in the bondage of Egypt. God asks Moses to deliver his people from slavery.

Moses is confused by the content and demands of worshiping God. How can he rise to meet the needs of such acts of deliverance? God assures Moses that he is the God who acts in history. He will be with Moses in the jaws of trials. The result of this worship encounter is that Moses is transformed from herdsman to an instrument of God's love as he delivers the people from oppression.

This story suggests that authentic worship leads to *action* on the part of God's people to perform the will of God. Our salvation history guides us in our responsibility to provide authentic and creative worship that excites and extends the responsibility of the believer.

THE CHALLENGE FOR US

We may nod in agreement with these traditional thoughts while quietly slipping into assuming that the most predictable and comfortable methods of worship are the best. To the contrary. The practice of doing things the way we always have is dangerous. It is easy to confuse nostalgic attitudes with the historical perspective.

Young or old, we are tempted to embrace only what we have experienced. We take this limited view and rewrite the past. ("The *last* pastor picked the most beautiful Gospel hymns." Or, "Our *last* youth leader could play the most wonderful music on her guitar.") This selective recall of our personal experience tends to make today's worship pale in comparison. We are always trapped by this kind of wishful thinking.

On the other hand, the historical recall of experience is based solidly on the acts of our forebears in faith. This means that we can draw upon 4,000 years of varied worship moments.

In the course of this historical span, God's people permitted the Spirit to create worship events that called upon all the senses. For instance, the celebration which led to the founding of the church (Acts 2) was a highly physical worship service. All of the believers were gathered in one place. Their ears and eyes became a means to experience the presence of God. They *felt* the Holy Spirit fall upon them. Wondrous acts of the Spirit in the lives of people and in nature were not uncommon in these early Christian services. Indeed, if you can think of some new way of worship, it usually means that you are not aware of our complete liturgical history. Somewhere, sometime, God's people probably have offered praise to God in a similar manner.

History does not limit us; rather, it compels us to let our faith determine fresh and exciting forms for worship. I acknowledge that we should regard the worship rituals and forms of our past with respect. Our personal history is important and real. Yet, the God of salvation history continues to act and move in our midst. We are not inventing our faith as we live. We are called to build upon our special legacy. It is our responsibility to assist the thrust of past faithfulness as we worship in the present and in the future.

You may come from a tradition that regards certain forms of worship very seriously. The liturgical churches

focus on beautiful language and music. The so-called
"free" churches also have many preserved forms. Just try
to change the order of service and take the offering earlier
or later than usual and you will hear more than one critical
comment.

The exciting journey of worship which you are about
to undertake honors both styles of tradition. We are called
to work within these legacies to touch God's people with
fresh meaning.

A NEW CREATION IN CHRIST

The word "creative" seems so natural to me. It wasn't
always this way. I have not been endowed with the gifts
usually associated with creativity such as singing, dancing,
drawing or playing an instrument. Only through my
growth as a Christian have I come to understand my creativity as a special aspect of God's love. We are new creations in Christ.

Each of us who is baptized into Christ is a creative
being. Christ has taken the old being and made us a new
person in him. This newness enables us to bring together
all the segments of our existence into a new, meaningful
and authentic whole. This act of "getting it together" is a
premiere act of creativity. Even the graphic or musical
artist puts together elements which have previously existed.

Being a creative Christian means that we are called to
strive for a wholistic approach to life—in fellowship, study,
outreach and worship. This book provides many creative
ideas. But it is your task to create meaningful worship
experiences for youth and adults. The task is not over-
whelming as long as you take seriously the fact that you
are a new creation in Christ.

You can see that I have a great deal of confidence in
you. I know that God will lead you in a special way to provide the best possible exciting and authentic worship
events.

The risk of letting the Spirit lead you to a different
kind of worship experience creates discomfort in every
youth group leader or worship committee. After 35 years of
working with youth, I am still frightened when a group of
teenagers and I offer a fresh way to worship. Perhaps this

fear is only natural. We are not called to be comfortable; we are called to be faithful. The content of the Gospel is risky. To face our God in direct conversation is an awe-filled moment! The form of expressing it can be no less demanding.

By planning creative worship experiences for youth groups, you also can renew worship for all ages in the congregation. The old as well as the young need the special energy and insight of fresh worship forms. Young people have a special ministry to the whole people of God. Worship may be the most important area for the youth to make a contribution.

THE WORSHIP STORYBOARD

There are dozens of ideas for worship in this book. Friends, young and old, have shared them with me. I have divided the worship service into segments in order to clearly present these new ideas. I also have chosen this approach because I want you to choose the most authentic call to enable your young people to worship. Only you are in a position to make this happen.

It is difficult to shape a living form like liturgy. It is particularly difficult to use the traditional approach of developing a linear "order" which lists consecutive actions.

The best "order" I can share is the one which has developed out of my work as a radio and television writer/producer. People creating these highly complex media messages commonly use a "storyboard." The usual storyboard reports on paper that which is happening in both sound and sight. The format often includes a split page with drawings on the left and audio on the right. This helps production people and talent to create the intention of the writers.

The storyboard helps us to include a number of important things in worship. For example, in the biblical picture of worship we have the sensual involvement of the people praising God (smell, incense; touch, healing; sight, the burning bush; hearing, music, voices; tasting, the bread and the cup). There is also a setting in which all this takes place (outdoors, upper room, temple, prison, etc.). Corporate celebration involves a number of people with different needs, levels of understanding and roles. Worship also has a specific content. God gathers the people of faith in order to have them hear and respond to the Word of truth.

I propose a special storyboard to help you in planning the format for the worship experience. Divide a legal-size sheet of paper into five columns. Label each of the columns: Word, People, Setting, Visual, Audio. (See illustration below.)

The Word	People	Setting	Visual	Audio

The flow of the service will deal with each of the columns. For instance, start with the call to worship. What scripture will you use (Word)? Who will be at the worship (People)? In what special area would you like to meet (Setting)? Are there unique props you'll need (Visual)? Will you use music (Audio)? Work on each of the columns to describe how you are going to handle this opening part of the service. Let's look at the purpose of each of the five columns.

THE WORD COLUMN

There is a given content to the act of worship: God. This column is the safeguard of authenticity as you design creative worship opportunities.

It is easy to be seduced by wonderful media forms. God works through all things. This means that Jesus can lead us to an idea without our complete understanding of how we thought of it. Intuition is one of the more consistent ways that God speaks to us. If Christ is in us, the thoughts within us are from him. Yet our own minds aid us in the quest for truth. I have found that my intuition works the best when I have prepared intellectually and experientially.

Develop this column in order to stay rooted in the content of worship. Note the reasons why you were led to make a particular choice.

THE PEOPLE COLUMN

Who are the receivers of the Word? This question is one of the most important learnings from Jesus' example. His forms of communication seem to shift vastly at different points in the Gospels: He told stories, carried on dialogues, rebuked, and just let people touch him. Jesus adjusted his proclamation so that people could encounter him in the way they needed. God became flesh in Jesus Christ so that we might better know him. This was the only way that we could grasp his message of salvation.

It becomes very important that you stand in the shoes of the worshipers. You are trying to help people meet the living God.

In the rest of this column, write a couple sentences to remind yourself of the composition of the congregation (age, different school districts, how well they know each other, etc.), recent events (mill closes, school loses big game, etc.), and their expectations (first time for creative worship—do they know that it will be different?). In the rest of the column, note the involvement and movement of the congregation during the worship.

THE SETTING COLUMN

Youth worship is unique, because it easily can be held in fresh and exciting settings. (I will probe this dimension of worship in a following chapter.) We are not only called to choose the right setting for worship, but we also must be prepared to utilize it well. Most assembly halls and sanctuaries are not used to their full potential for worship. The environment doesn't have to remain static. In fact, most worship settings have special contributions to make which are overlooked. For instance, the glass, wood, brick and stone of the building are opportunities to draw people closer to the Word of God. In the worship, include moments for people to feel, see and study these elements.

In this column, write directions to help you keep the function of the setting fully before you. Include the sensual aspects of worship which are not covered under the last two columns, i.e., smell, taste, touch.

THE VISUAL COLUMN

An old hymn pleads that God might open our eyes. Worship is an opportunity to help us see God's love and truth. We live in a world that exploits sight through television, video and film. Yet, most worship does very little to enhance understanding through this special gift of sight.

This column focuses on the windows, banners, bulletins, liturgy, special dress of leaders and many more visual aspects of celebration. You can draw pictures in this column to further clarify aspects of the worship. At what points will the people be led to focus on a particular visual aspect of the service? There may be points when the worshipers close their eyes.

THE AUDIO COLUMN

Contemporary people have been raised on superb sound production in the media. When a prayer circle is designed in such a way so that people cannot hear each other, there is a loss in the corporate nature of worship.

This column contains the parts to be read or sung by the leaders. Working on this aspect of the service also will help you become aware of how silence can play an important role in worship.

Adjust this storyboard concept for your own needs. You will notice that lining up the different aspects of worship in this flow sheet will enable you to see the relationship between the parts of the service. In fact, the practice of looking at the whole service will help you create new ideas.

These basic thoughts about the theology of worship and the practical way of organizing the service will be developed as we move through this book. I have chosen to dissect the worship service in a way which may or may not bear the same names as your traditional service; don't be confused by any differences. I have found the basic elements of worship chosen for discussion in this book appear in every Christian service.

Welcome to a wonderful journey of faith!

CHAPTER 2

The Walls of Resistance to Creative Worship

The youth and I had worked long and hard on the youth Sunday service. They had collected 150 small stones from the church's parking lot and drawn a small cross on each one. How would the congregation, mostly adults, respond to this unusual communion service? One elder stopped to talk to me after the service. "Dennis, I didn't get anything out of what you and the kids did, but keep at it."

I think that I was happier with Jack's frank comment than I would have been with empty praise. He was being honest, but he wasn't attacking or trying to hurt us. His Christian love permitted him to be open with and supportive of us. Before we share ideas for creative worship, we need to discuss what can be done in the face of resistance.

Unfortunately, many young people have been degraded and hurt when they have introduced unfamiliar worship forms in traditional settings. There is often an unhealthy method of resisting worship changes in many congregations. These negative critics of the new forms don't confront the young people or their leaders directly. Rumors are often passed second-hand to those in charge. The criticism magnifies itself until it seems everyone believes what is probably the opinion of just one or two people. This gossip often breeds anger and disappointment among the young people who have worked to add a meaningful contribution to the act of glorifying God. By hearing gossip, rumors and negative comments from a few people, it is easy for the youth to assume that the whole church is against them.

There is no aspect of the local congregation's life where criticism can arise so easily as worship. The Apostle Paul was forced to deal with abusive behavior during worship in the same churches he founded in his missionary travels. The early church fathers also were outspoken about Christians who distorted worship with immorality. Even the Christians of frontier America were torn by such controversies as whether or not to use the organ in worship.

Your church and other Christians in the community may feel tension and conflict when change comes to their worship experiences. Whether the service substitutes English for another language or moves the location of the choir, people may express their unhappiness. It is understandable why Christians are particularly touchy about altering the order of worship. There is a skin-close relationship between the structure of worship and our personal faith.

We are drawn to worship for a number of different reasons. The simplest service and the most elaborate liturgical service are *both* revered to the smallest detail by the believer. We come from the confusion and instability of the world to find a sense of continuity and stability in worship.

Ted Gill, noted theologian and Christian writer, once said that the church originally was a rescue mission, but now it is a comfort station. We find a certain security in its familiar rhythms, just as a small child feels a certain security in lining up her stuffed animals in an exact order each night. God is gracious in meeting our needs for symbols, words, songs and other points of reference in our worship. This means that people are more likely to accept boredom from an old form than be challenged on a foreign liturgical terrain. Yet, Ted Gill is correct about the original thrust of the faith community: The God we worship calls us to a ministry which rescues, resurrects, restores, renews and recommits.

I think that some people seek a sense of forgiveness and cleansing through the boredom of the service! By enduring something unpleasant and irrelevant, they seem to gain the impression that they have earned forgiveness. Of course, only Christ forgives. We cannot earn what is already given through grace. A relevant, demanding and creative service easily can be a disappointment or a disgrace for people with such needs.

The violation of an expectation upsets most people. An outraged elderly church member is not complaining over the slides shown in the service because he doesn't understand media. As a matter of fact, the elderly member is very media conscious. He watches more slick media techniques in 10 hours of television a day than a teenager does. The elderly church member is shaking his fist at the minister because his covenant of expectation was broken.

For many years, I have struggled with walls of resistance. I have discovered seven insights that help meet this potential conflict with Christian love and creative sensitivity.

1. Create a covenant of expectation. It is important to establish a new contract of expectation with the congregation. This must be done in such a way so the people are not frightened by what is coming. Simply give them a preparatory notice and an explanation of the new service.

For example, one team of pastors worked with the youth to create six very unusual worship services for the weeks leading up to Easter. Instead of apologizing for the radical changes or surprising the congregation, the worship team widely advertised the special Lenten celebrations. They informed the members of how the services were built on the historical services of the church. They encouraged the community to invite friends. The evangelism and outreach emphases appealed to many who would have been reduced to complaints if the leadership team hadn't been so sensitive and caring. You can guess what happened: Attendance reached an all-time high for the season and the team was urged to make it an annual series.

2. Create a support system. The natural resistance to creative worship can only be faced in a loving way as a team effort. Too often a youth director will pass out speaking parts to several youth and hope that the youth Sunday will work. A *team* needs to probe the worship experience together in order to form a worship flow that reflects God's Word.

I have never met a person who can consistently produce creative worship experiences alone. The key to creative worship leadership is to gather a team of youth to support and help in the task.

Such a community effort will reap more ideas and support for risking. Criticism can be handled much more lovingly when your team stands with you. Anger and hostility appear in the leader who must face disappointment alone. The context for the work of the Holy Spirit as comforter is the community of the faithful.

One pastor provided the ultimate support team. He created a worship committee which changed membership every two weeks! In the course of two years, he had several people serve on this team including both adults and young people. Criticism and resistance totally disappeared as a result of the educational process of such a set-up.

3. Nurture a feedback system. The faith community often works on a very unsatisfactory feedback system. Only those who complain receive attention from the clergy and ruling board. Criticism then becomes the way to take matters seriously. It is the squeaking wheel that gets the grease of attention.

In many settings, there is a tyranny of singular critics. We encourage a pathological system of care. Rumors of a person's unhappiness can terrorize many clergy. My wife, Marilyn, would get a phone call after church. The person would tell Marilyn that she had overheard someone else who was very angry about something the youth had said or done at worship! We would sometimes spend the rest of the day trying to figure out who was unhappy about what. This meant that we were totally ignoring the people who found the worship meaningful.

We developed a more helpful model to change this negative dynamic. After the youth-oriented services, the young people would invite the congregation to attend a coffee hour at which the youth served their homemade goodies. As the people entered our social hall, the youth passed out blank cards, asking the people to write comments about what had happened to them spiritually during worship. Please note that we did *not* ask them to write about what they liked or didn't like. I don't believe that this is a proper question for Christians. We don't come to worship for our pleasure; we come to worship the living God.

The young people then called the group to order and collected the unsigned cards. I had trained the youth to conduct the energy offered by the people and not to defend or explain the service. They started reading the cards. When they came to a negative comment, the moderator asked other people in the room to share how they reacted to this opinion. Of course, there were always people who liked what another person didn't like.

One Sunday, a negative comment on a card about "the loud music" was answered by the oldest person in the room. "I enjoyed hearing the music for a change!" Who would think this conservative lady would be supportive? This type of process gives the critic a chance to be heard and places the negative comment in the proper perspective of a minority opinion. The young people also learned how to deal with criticism in a Christian context.

Most people with critical opinions become angry when they think that they are not being heard. When people have an honest chance to express themselves, they are partially satisfied. There is often misunderstanding at the base of criticism over worship. When lovingly challenged about the need for a change, most Christians will rise to the occasion and be very generous.

4. Affirm continuity. It is vital to take seriously the historical context of your weekly service. Many youth services tend to change everything. There are no handles by which the traditional worshiper can get an emotional grip. The totally transformed service totally disorients the faithful.

It is wise to work within the given framework of the service. Try to enrich each part of the worship order with fresh and authentic means of celebration. The worshiper is then able to follow the continuity from the past. For example, a group of young people and I were conducting an "outer space" worship service for a group of liturgically sensitive adults. We followed the regular order; however, after each part of the service we provided a "space age" name.

5. Nurture positive adult attitudes toward youth. The role of the adults, advisers or leaders is extremely important in the quest to overcome adult resistance to creative worship. One loving youth worker, Ruth, told me that most churches don't have very high opinions of their youth. She was aware of this problem in her church. Ruth loved the young people and knew that they were very special. She undertook an intentional campaign to let the other adults know how neat their youth were. Whenever she talked with other adults, she always added some honest opinions about their fine young people.

Christians need to affirm one another consistently and honestly. Many youth groups and adults have developed a continuous series of "put-downs" with each other. This practice is not funny and undermines the freedom of mutual trust between the young and the old.

6. Introduce changes slowly. A church-official friend, Harold, likes to talk about the practice used by horse trainers. Harold says that horses don't like being broken in to the saddle. Wise trainers will hang the horse blanket in the stall for several weeks until the horse is accustomed to the item which it will eventually wear. Harold is sure that people behave in the same way: "You got to hang the blanket for a while." Change in worship can be embraced only when people have experienced the validity of new forms. It is unfair to ask young people what they want to do without giving them an option. It is also impossible for adults to surrender accustomed ways of worship for new modes without the experience.

Many churches open their worship to the ideas and energy of youth by creating a special weekly "youth" or "family" service. This optional worship experience draws many people. As the service gains acceptance, innovations start to develop. A number of congregations have found that the "family" celebrations draw more people than the usual worship service!

7. Draw upon prayer for wisdom. Prayer is the ultimate context for the creative response to resistance. This is more than just praying for your opponents. The source of creative ideas is the Holy Spirit. The language of a creative community is conversation with God. We are called to pray for those who resist us. For young people, prayer is vital; it will put opposition in a whole different realm. Don't go to prayer alone in the midst of resistance. Draw upon your support system; pray for those who oppose you and misunderstand what the youth are trying to accomplish.

THEOLOGICAL FOUNDATIONS FOR CHANGE

There is also a serious theological source of misunderstanding and resistance to change in worship. Many people look at worship as if it is a private, pietistic experience. This individualistic model means that the worshiper is only concerned with his or her needs. I know there is wide narcissism in our culture; yet Christ calls his church as a community of faith.

One Sunday, an elderly person approached me. She was very unhappy about the choice of hymns. (I had been including contemporary hymns in each service.) After listening to her unhappiness, I shared with her the reasons behind my choice. We had several young people who were new to the faith; they had no history of worship in the church. I wanted to give them a taste of a music style closer to their experience. She looked at me for a few seconds. "You mean that by permitting one of those new songs, I am actually helping a young person grow in the faith?" I nodded to her. "I never thought about it in that way. I guess worship is giving as well as receiving." Of course, she never resisted my changes again. This dear person just needed to see worship as an inclusive event in which many people are fed.

Likewise, when the young people criticized the old Gospel hymns I included each week, I told them about a particular person in the congregation who loved them. The youth eventually surrendered their criticism to give her something of meaning.

We are known to the world by the way we love each other. Christian love is focused in intimacy and sharing. The act of worship is one of the most intimate experiences we share with others. We do not worship selfishly. It is important that others around us also are being drawn into a conversation with God.

This theology of worship is the foundation of all that is presented in this book. Even when we are isolated in hospitals or jails, worship moments are in the presence of the communion of saints. The Holy Spirit assures us that our relationship to Christ is both vertical and horizontal. We raise our hands to God, but they are joined with those around us.

THE PASTOR AND CHANGE

In recent years, I have revised my opinion of the role played by pastors in youth ministry. I used to skip over pastors and just focus on youth advisers and workers. The pastor is often the wall of resistance to creative worship. When I discover an exciting worship life in a local congregation, there is usually an enabling pastor in the background. Some clergy can provide leadership in this area, but some pastors encourage others to fill this role such as a youth worker or volunteer.

A few years ago, I was in Australia and some friends urged me to travel 150 miles in the early morning to attend a "family" worship at a church. This was an amazing experience. A husband and wife team led 175 people of all ages in a worship event through which we followed Moses in the wilderness.

After the regular service, I ate lunch at the minister's house. He seemed to be a bland and unexciting man. "I know that the early service is more worshipful than the 11 a.m. worship; I could never do what Mel and Betty do. Yet, I am so proud of their ministry." I realized that this pastor was an outstanding man. He had nurtured and encouraged these people to provide that creative service. For the sake of meaningful worship for his congregation, he was willing to step back and allow others to lead. His authentic character of ministry is needed much more in the local congregation.

When I tell this story to people in workshops, I am told about how different their pastor is. "What can we do? He (or she) discourages change for young people." There is no easy answer for this wall of resistance, yet it is a situation that must be faced by the adult advisers. You are the advocate for youth. They need your work on their behalf.

I have found that most resistant pastors to creative worship are those who were not prepared in seminary to think creatively. And then when they get out in the field, their lack of creative training often gets them in trouble, Many of these people *never* receive affirmation in the congregation when they do risk. Young people can do a great deal by supporting the pastor in his or her growth in worship leadership. I suggest two ways by which a pastor can grow in handling creative worship.

First, urge the pastor to gather four or five young people who are out on the edge of worship. These may be the teenagers who hang out in the doughnut shop or stand in the parking lot during Sunday morning services. Have the pastor invite the youth to a discussion on worship. The youth may honestly admit that worship is pretty boring. The pastor can relate how he or she wants it changed, but doesn't know how to do it. The pastor also can admit honest feelings such as fear of adult reactions. Encourage the pastor to ask these young people to help for the next couple months as the changes are made. The youth will see a pastor who is an authentic person. The pastor will develop a fresh source of energy and ideas from this support group.

Teenagers often see only adults who are "completed" instead of "becoming." This makes the chasm in spiritual growth between the young and the old wider than it really is.

Second, those who preach (lay or clergy) should find a communication mentor to help them improve. Consider this reality: Pastors often have no sounding board for support, suggestions and growth. Everyone needs an "ear" to listen and a friend to be there.

Find a program director of a local radio or television station. It will be best if he or she is not a Christian or a church member. (The church seems to blunt the creative gifts of people when they apply their art to the church.) Approach this person and ask if he or she will critique your message over a four-week period as if you were an employee at the station. Buy the program director breakfast each morning as you are critiqued. You will be amazed how much you will grow in terms of communication skills. By the way, the media person also will be touched by a Christian who humbly receives the tutoring of another.

THE FAULT LIES NOT IN OUR OPPONENTS, BUT WITHIN OURSELVES

Shakespeare may not have appreciated my above paraphrase of his famous line. However, he was right in suggesting that we cannot blame others for the resistance which we may face. As I have suggested, the people who resist innovation in worship are not evil or wrong. They have very important needs and will oppose change when they are not helped.

When we are frightened at times of risk, it is tempting to take an attitude of superiority. People may resist this defensiveness rather than the actual ideas! Question yourself about how you deal with the fear of leading creative worship.

Sometimes people tell me that their youth program suffers from the lack of creativity because "we are a conservative church." This is ridiculous. The conservative Christian can be the best supporter of worship innovation. He or she must be won through love and reason. If you can demonstrate your authenticity, enthusiasm and biblical roots, conservative Christians will support you. The wonderful gift from my conservative friends is that they stay with me longer than "liberal" people. If they do not support you, you either have a bad idea or they don't understand you.

Resistance to change in worship also can be found within your youth group. Remember that children are the product of adult worship. Most young people are very traditional when they are given control to guide worship.

I remember a time in Michigan when the service was turned over to a group of 600 young people. They could have done the service any way they desired. One group of young people had the call to worship. Their creative idea was to bring in the other students in groups of 20 and make them sit on the floor in perfect rows—just like pews!

They only knew what they had experienced. They were merely acting out the impact of adult attitudes in worship. Again, experience is the key to change within young people's worship.

In authentic Christian worship, the Holy Spirit removes any walls which separate brothers and sisters of faith. The worship event is the moment when Christ enables us to be the kinship of God. The only real walls of resistance are created by us. It is not the new worship idea or the change of the traditional which brings criticism. The amount we prepare ourselves, our ideas and the worshiper determines the openness or resistance to our creative efforts.

A school encouraged its teachers to create innovative ways to teach reading. Whenever an instructor offered a fresh method to his or her students, the results were fantastic. However, when the department adopted the approach to be used by other teachers, the results fell back to the previous level. It was concluded that the initiating teacher's enthusiasm was the major factor in the students improved performance. The same dynamics are present in creative worship changes. It is your love and excitement which will pave the way for others to accept the flow of worship innovation.

The spirit of expectation needs to overwhelm the person preparing for the leadership of creative worship. You are preparing the way of the Lord for his people! Carry this level of hope with you as you accept the wonderfully demanding task of seeking new wineskins for this special wine of life: worship.

CHAPTER 3

The Setting for Worship

"Have faith, will travel." God has called the faithful to worship in every possible setting. The Bible offers a variety of settings for worship (tents, temples, hillsides, common rooms, jails, etc.). Contemporary people also have praised God in caves, death-row cells, on mountaintops and under the sea in submarines. Every moment of life provides fitting occasions for worship. There is no improper setting for praising and serving God. Worship is our chief reason for existing. We are to glorify and enjoy God forever, everywhere.

It is helpful to recognize special places in order for us to acknowledge fully the "otherness" in the midst of the "newness" which takes place in worship. Just as Moses experienced God's presence along the shepherd's trail, so God works in our lives *today*. The secular and the sacred are inseparable through God's presence within each of us.

Our approach to worship is a most important guide in determining the proper setting. There have been improper worship experiences in great sacred buildings; and there have been majestic worship celebrations in common places. It is not the location which makes the difference in authenticity. The Spirit of God determines the validity of worship. How do we choose the setting which enables us to communicate with God?

Designing youth worship gives us special freedom. There are five excellent reasons why new worship settings are possible and necessary.

First, youth groups usually meet at a nontraditional worship time and setting. It is not necessarily expected that you will use the adult place of worship. Most members of the youth group have already worshiped with the congregation at a Sunday morning gathering. There is a supplementary role assigned to many youth worship events. This can be a great disadvantage. The youth may not take their own worship very seriously. On the other hand, the chance that your service will be very special to them in a more intimate setting is also most likely.

Second, youth ministry often takes you to different settings in the course of your programming (retreats, workcamps, retirement homes, etc.). There is a natural quality to worshiping in a different place other than the traditional worship area. The tasks of serving, fellowship and studying strongly imply that worship be included at the place where the events are taking place.

Third, the service is usually directed toward the youth group. They often have a stronger sense of fellowship and security than do adults. The young people can be freed to accept a new setting for worship. They usually wear comfortable clothes and can fit into any setting. The floor or a grassy field will be acceptable places for young people.

Fourth, the senses are a very important part of the youth group's exploration and discovery of the world. The teenager may not put everything into his or her mouth like a crawling baby, but he or she is very aware of the sensual dimensions of the physical and emotional setting. This is the best preparation for receivers of the Word who worship in a new setting. They will naturally touch, taste, smell, listen and see the context of celebrating God's love.

Finally, most youth worship events are small. This means that feedback and participation are easy to nurture. If a different setting does not aid in praising God, you will know this immediately. When we accept the freedom for worship in any setting, we are overwhelmed with a new awareness of God's presence in every facet of life.

CHOOSING THE SETTING

If you have a choice about where you are going to hold worship, exercise this opportunity in planning your service. There is a link between our physical location (or space in creation) and God's calling in our lives. Worship in a special location provides a unique opportunity to probe such meanings for our lives.

Here are six guidelines for choosing a site or setting for creative youth worship. These guidelines are quite basic to all of life: the five senses plus one.

1. Eyes. I still remember a view from a worship experience which was held on a high cliff overlooking the surf in Australia. Yet, it is often difficult to "behold" the space in which we are to worship God. We accept the notion that buildings used for worship are mere shells of protection against bad weather or buffers against outside distractions. We are called to worship with all our senses. All things contribute to our focus on God's grace.

Look over the setting you are considering. Are there special places within the space which can be used for certain parts of the service? There is no reason why the worshipers can't move during the course of the celebration. How does the presence or the absence of light suggest opportunities to present different aspects of the service? The space will open before you as you view it through eyes of faith.

2. Ears. The Australian worship service overlooking the ocean filled more than my eyes. The pounding of the surf became a majestic rhythm for our prayers.

The place you are considering offers unique opportunities to hear the sounds of faith. There are rooms which carry a whisper to the farthest point from the speaker. There also are rooms with bad acoustics where you can't hear a word of the prayer offered by a brother or sister. You may be limited in some ways considering how much the worshipers can share. On the other hand, you may find that the aural character will suggest special ways to worship God.

3. Nose. Every place has a special odor. My mother believes that all church buildings have a special smell. As you survey a setting for worship, consider what your nose tells you about this service. Does the aroma of flowers or freshly cut grass drift into this place? What does this suggest about the prayers of thanksgiving that may be offered? Perhaps you will want to enrich the place by introducing odors such as flowers and incense.

4. Touch. Worship has often limited the use of our hands. We are invited to listen, but not touch. Walk around your potential worship space and feel the walls. Is there a sense of the "wailing wall" in Jerusalem? Could the cracks and lines suggest suffering and pain if you used touch in your service?

Be sensitive to the feeling of the floor. Is it sand or stone? Could carpeting be used to have a barefooted worship experience? The pews or other seating places also can give you tactile ideas for worship. There may be a special feel to the wood or metal.

Consider whether this space will lend itself to the use of touch among the members. Some seating arrangements restrict movement and opportunities for touch.

5. Taste. No, I will not suggest that you taste the space! Yet, how does this space affect the breaking of bread together? The disciples found a room where they could celebrate the Passover. Many settings restrict sharing and community. Does the space permit breaking of bread with those who will worship?

6. Intuition: the Holy Spirit. How does the worship setting "feel" to you? Can you relive moments of its previous use? How will God use this setting so that the people may worship? I urge you to permit a "non-rational" flow of the other guidelines to blend into your own emotional system. I have found myself saying aloud, "God, how do you want me to use this setting to glorify you?"

If we are in Christ, we can trust the quiet and unexplainable ways he works on us in worship. My biggest mistakes resulted from my failure to listen to what I have intuitively known to be right. I have let my mind talk me out of doing what I should have done. There is a heavy responsibility in loving and following God. It is so easy to let the self override the voice of the Spirit. Let the blending of these clues lead you in choosing and utilizing special settings for worship.

The following 10 settings have been particularly meaningful to those who utilized them. These testimonies are given to encourage you to respond to the Spirit who is working within you. May these creative environments inspire you to explore the sites around you.

JAIL

The two teenagers and their college-age leader were very nervous. None of them had ever been in jail. The three were ushered back into the dirty and dark confines of the old county jail. The guard surprised them with the order, "The men go this way and the woman that way." They had assumed that they would have each other for support as they led worship. The male leader was awe-struck by the courage of 17-year-old Donna, who calmly went alone into the women's section. She was willing to tackle the task of leading worship by herself.

Some of the men gathered around when the other two announced that they would worship God together. The leader and teenager couldn't help but feel the impact of this environment. What had first seemed so unappealing and disgraceful slowly revealed to them a special character. As they read the passage about the Apostle Paul's imprisonment, they realized that this space was giving them a true biblical context for worship.

The youth leader watched one man who had stayed in his bunk and refused to join them. The man got up and walked over to the open toilet. He proceeded to use it as the leader read the opening Bible passage. The prisoner then returned to his bunk and flopped down with a heavy sigh.

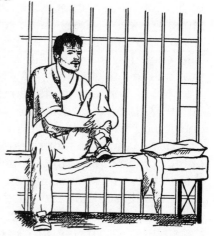

As the service continued, the leader noticed a slow change in the prisoner's attitude toward them. His eyes no longer focused on the ceiling. He was being drawn into the power of the worship service! He could relate to the prisoner Paul. As the worship leaders shook hands with the men at the end of the service, the resistant prisoner approached the youth worker. The prisoner placed his hand on the youth worker's shoulder. "God understands. You understand. Thank you."

After the service, as the youth leader and two teenagers reflected on their frightening and moving experience, they discovered that the setting actually provided an important dimension to the worship. They had received as much from the prison service as did the prisoners.

NATURE

Dave was bubbling over. He had just returned from his second trip to troubled Central America. "It was the most moving experience I had ever encountered in worship. Our group of 14 was in a rural village. We gathered on a hill just outside the community. Our little circle of people joined hands and prayed.

"We could feel the land and its people; hear the sounds of nature; smell the aroma of breakfast being prepared; and see the sparkle of the foliage. Suddenly, we knew that something had changed. The insects and birds stopped making their special sounds. I looked up and saw about 20 teenagers emerging from the woods just a few feet to our left. They wore battle dress and carried machine guns! We knew about these ruthless troops. Several Americans had been killed by armed fighters such as these. The guerrillas surrounded our circle. A member of our group asked in Spanish, 'Will you join us in worship?'

"Time seemed to stand still. One young man, not over 16 or 17 nodded to the others. They then stepped forward and joined us in worship!"

Dave's story is more dramatic than most of our own outdoor worship settings. However, nature provides one of the best and most exciting environments for creative worship. Don't feel that you need the most dramatic outdoor settings; simply use the church's back yard, the park down the street or a parking lot. You'll be surprised at how much will be added to your youth worship.

CAVE

One of my friends, Kit, found that his region featured an extensive network of caves which were opened to the public. Kit arranged to hold an overnight retreat in one of these caves for his junior high group. If you have ever been in a cave, you know the darkness there is the most intense of all places. There is something frightening about being in total darkness.

Kit led the junior high youth in a very meaningful worship experience which drew upon the history of the early church's use of caves for worship. He led them through a guided fantasy, taking them back to the early Christians who hid from the Romans in caves.

The service went on for a long time. The students allowed the cave to give them a very special perspective about the comfort God gives in the midst of life's darknesses.

LOW-TRAFFIC CHURCH SPACES

Every church has special places which are behind closed doors. In some buildings this may be a furnace room or storage area. These places are dark and away from the usual paths of traffic.

One youth group was studying the Gospel of John and its contrasting use of light and darkness. The students were led into the dark furnace room. The entire service was conducted in this space with the use of a small candle. During the prayer time, the candle was passed around the circle and each student shared how the light of Christ came into his or her life.

Your weekly youth worship service will be enriched by seeking such unfamiliar places. Another way to take advantage of "hidden" spaces in the church for worship is for the intreat (or lock-in). This home-based model utilizes the local church as the setting for an overnight retreat. One junior high group had a very meaningful worship experience in the darkened building. The members had to silently find each hidden person and gather the community for worship. It was a hide-and-seek call to worship in the setting of a dark church building!

Another group of young people worshiped in the bell

tower. They were able to use this environment for prayers and other parts of their service. At one point, they each looked out a different window at the surrounding country-side. The youth shared their reflections on what things would make Jesus weep if he looked at this community today.

HOMES

The use of homes for youth worship is one of the most obvious, yet most often overlooked settings. Parachurch youth movements have long utilized this location for their programming. Indeed, the early church used homes for worship.

The home has the great advantage over the use of a church building by providing a special opportunity for intimacy. This is a particularly important setting for small youth groups. The huge church basement with only five people makes worship seem unpopular and lonely.

Both those at the birth of the church (Acts 2:1-4) and the leaders of parachurch youth movements have found that the Spirit touches believers most frequently when people are gathered together in a tight space. The limited space forces the community to touch and share in a special way. Love feasts and the breaking of bread come most naturally in such settings.

VEHICLES

Many groups take trips in the course of their life together. The traveling groups provide one of the most exciting opportunities for worship. For instance, one youth group had a traveling worship service. They stopped at a different place for each part of the celebration. The prayer of thanksgiving was experienced by a beautiful stream. Each person was asked to wander in silence for a few minutes in the midst of this beauty. The youth were asked to find something for which they felt thankful to God and bring that item back to the worship center. The actual prayer consisted of their offerings of beauty. One person returned with nothing. When his turn came to share, he told the group about the gift of God he had found in a flower. However, he did not want to disturb the flower, so he left it where God had put it so that others might enjoy this gift.

Another group of young people focused on the sermon as they traveled in their van. The text dealt with the road to Emmaus where the disciples' eyes were opened to Christ when they invited him to eat with them. Revelation and hospitality were interlocked. The leader suddenly stopped and picked up a person who was hitchhiking along the road. For the next hour, the youth talked with this stranger. After he left, the youth shared how he had opened the passage to their understanding.

Imagine how enriched your journey can become by using the trip itself as your setting for worship.

NURSING HOMES AND CARE FACILITIES

One of the most misused settings for worship is the nursing facility. There is the temptation to entertain the old. Many people don't understand how important it is for those with limited control over their lives to participate actively in something. Singing is not always the best way for the old to be part of the worship. Many of these people simply don't have enough wind to sing.

Yet, the care facility may be one of the most important places for the young and old to glorify God in worship. For example, well-known clown minister Floyd Shaffer provides a worship service which draws everyone into the historical liturgy. He was working at a nursing home with his teenage clowns. They came to the part of the service where each person receives "the mark of the clown." This emotional moment offers the worshiper a chance to receive a small spot of clown makeup on his or her cheek.

Floyd stopped before an elderly woman who was confined to a wheelchair. He gave her the mark. When he stepped back, she stood up and walked toward him. The woman threw her arms around him and gave him a great hug. She then sat again in the chair.

After the event, the director remarked on how amazing the service was. Floyd said that he had felt "electric" energy pass through him when the woman hugged him. The director shook his head. "It was amazing. You know, she hasn't walked in three years."

The key to utilizing the nursing home is to enable the residents to participate in the service. What is it that they can give in worship? They certainly have their stories and witnesses to offer.

WORKCAMPS AND MISSION SETTINGS

This kind of service is one of the most important aspects of youth ministry. So many lives have been changed in the process of Christian service to others. These camps are often held in areas which need basic home improvement, church teachers or other forms of aid. Servanthood is an excellent theme for the worship services in this setting. For the worship experiences, it is particularly important to draw upon the greatest resource of these places: the local people who are being served.

Your youth also will bear physical marks of their service. They may be tired, blistered and insect-bitten. How can the feelings caused by hard work be used at worship? The youth can tell of their struggles as they serve. They also can share the gifts and insights the residents have shown to them. The young people can describe the memories that they will take back home with them.

The environmental setting of restored buildings, wilderness and poverty suggests many important clues to developing your worship time. Love feasts also have special meaning in these mission settings.

A friend of mine, Ed, was visiting a sister Baptist church during his stay in the Bahamas. The church of 20 members had invited the three Americans to a supper. They ate the special seafood of the islands and told many stories. At the concluding worship service, the visitors were led out in front of the rural church. While the young people sang an old Gospel hymn, each of the island Christians hugged the visitors. As the missionaries drove away, the island people kept singing a benediction for them. Ed says that he still can hear the gentle voices and feel the tears as these brothers and sisters in the faith faded from sight.

RETREATS

Just about every youth group slips away to a campsite

or other facility for a weekend retreat. What a wonderful setting for creative worship! There is the freedom to worship in almost any way you desire. The usual flow of life has been diverted.

I vividly remember my first retreat. I was a college student embarking on my first youth group leadership event. By some strange set of circumstances I ended up on a small island in Michigan with 25 teenagers and no other adults. Our food and energy supply broke down. We had to survive without water, toilet paper, lights and hot food. There was some mad behavior and a few dunkings in the cold lake. We had more peanut butter sandwiches than you can imagine. Yet the worship experiences in the cold around the fire were awesome.

We were emotionally drained after the first few hours of the retreat. I had masked my panic with angry words and threats. I had accused the guys with leather jackets of causing the power outage. I soon discovered that I was wrong. At our campfire, I asked the falsely accused rough guys for forgiveness. It was a stunning moment. Many tears and lots of hugs added something special to this worship setting. Our faith growth was lighted by stars at night and sparkling sun on the water in the morning.

Retreats can be exhausting. But I know of no other setting that offers as much opportunity for creative worship and spiritual growth in youth ministry.

SUNDAY MORNING—IN CHURCH

It is tempting to emphasize special unexpected or exotic settings in this book of creative worship options. However, Sunday morning is still a wonderful place for special worship moments. Earlier we discussed the special problems young people sometimes have in bringing change to this traditional setting. However, more creative things are happening on Sunday morning than at any other place in the life of the church! Drama, dance, special music, puppets, clowns, choral reading, slides and many other wonderful expressive ways to glorify God are being used by young people.

Sometimes even a small change can trigger much bigger renewal. One youth group was very unhappy about the climate of Sunday morning. They finally received permission to be the greeters at one door each week. On the first Sunday, the president of the group spoke to the congregation just before the benediction. She warned the worshipers to beware. "When you go out the front door, something strange and wonderful will happen to you. If you don't want to be hugged or given a balloon as a special way of saying that God loves you, please use another door."

Of course, you know what happened. The spirit of worship totally changed. The youth continued to be greeters. They discovered that the nearby funeral parlor always had extra flowers. They would collect these arrangements and remove the single flowers. On some Sundays, each person leaving by the "love door" would get a flower.

Please don't think that I have given up on Sunday mornings. That traditional service is still the flagship of all contemporary Christian celebration. But there are also many adults who crave lively and exciting worship. They just haven't experienced it yet.

God permits us to draw upon our spaces and settings for a wholistic experience of worship. The fact that youth can worship in unfamiliar spaces will help them realize that God calls us to worship at every point of our daily life. The very act of worship in another space will teach the vastness of God's lordship to all.

CHAPTER 4

The Call to Worship

God said, "Let there be light." And it was so.

The ram's horn sounds and the people make their way to the temple.

The bell rings and the people drop their tools as they walk to the old church.

The gun fires and the sprinters break from the blocks.

"4-3-2-1. Ignition." The space vehicle lifts from the pad.

We need points of departure to understand where we are and what we are about to pursue. Although we are called to worship God always, there is a conscious moment when we intentionally acknowledge that it is God with whom we are communicating.

Those who have followed God before us have used many ways to gather others for the intentional time of worship. Some have suggested that the Greek word for church means "to be called from" the world. I believe that such an interpretation of the word may be pushing it beyond its intention; however, it is an appropriate image. Christ calls us to refrain from our self-directed lives to glorify and enjoy God forever.

The most difficult demand on a call to worship is that it must result in the first step toward the gathering and forming of a community of faith. It is easy to assume that just because it is a set worship time, an authentic time of glorifying God will follow; this is not always true.

The context for the appearance of the Holy Spirit in the Bible is always the community of faith. It is true that Moses and others were physically alone when God spoke to them. Yet, each event was accompanied by God's acknowledgment that these people were called upon as part of the people of God. Moses was called from the worship event of the burning bush to accept his responsibility to the people held in captivity. God initiates the call, but it is the people of faith whom he beckons.

The sounding of the ram's horn or the church bell invites individuals to choose their identity as a kinship in Christ. This is not a natural or common commitment. Jesus Christ is the only source of such possibilities of kinship in the midst of diversity and separation. All walls separating social groups, age brackets and racial traditions have been removed by God's act of salvation in the Son.

The task of people designing the call to worship is to flesh out this theological promise. How can these isolated people become one body?

It is important that we follow biblical and historical clues in order to probe the many possibilities for beckoning Christians to our worship event. Following are three questions which provide guidelines for designing the call to worship.

1. Who are the people coming to the service? One needs to discover the worshipers. Of course, we all know the names and background of our youth. Yet, it is important to explore their expectations, needs and experiences. What do they personally bring to the worship service? For example, they may be coming from four different high schools and have different expectations for worship.

The physical development of the student is even an important insight. For example, if the students are young and lack in maturity, you should consider the need to have movement and physical activity. I used to teach a junior high class. One of my students would totally disrupt my class and worship service. He was a good kid; however, he was always punching or disturbing someone else. It was easy for me to respond to his need for physical activity by punishment. Fortunately, I stumbled upon a positive use of his energy. During class I had him fold bulletins. He could still contribute, but now he didn't have to hit someone to work out the pressures of his growing body. In the worship services, he was my assistant (ushering, taking the collection, etc.).

2. What is the world like from which they come? It is helpful to feel close to the immediate world from which the youth are called. What tools, activities or relationships are they leaving behind? A death of someone from school may set the entire mood for the service. What event in this world has made an impact on them during the past few hours?

The local hospital was alerted about an emergency at an elementary school a couple of years ago. Two hundred children had fainted! The medics administered first aid and rushed children to the hospital. They found that the young people recovered quickly and seemed to have no outward signs of illness. When authorities reconstructed the situation, they found that the children were unloading from the buses in front of the school. Someone said that he smelled something funny. It was at this point that the mass fainting took place.

An alert educator noted that there had been much publicity during the previous week concerning the development of a bomb which left buildings standing, but killed people. The young people were exposed to these stories on the "news breaks" for children during the cartoons. Was this a case of mass panic? an expression of their fear about a dangerous world? Your young people come from a world with many subtle influences. Worship planning needs to consider the influences of the world they leave in their quest to praise God.

3. What will God say to us at this time? It is our task to focus on what God has to say to us in the call to worship. We are accustomed to distilling our faith into three or four words. Yet, the whole spectrum of salvation history reveals that God offers us incredible avenues to find the connection between our personal life and the entire history of salvation. It is as if God offers us a wheel which has many different spokes. Each spoke leads to the center: God in Jesus Christ.

The wheel spins and stops at the very place where we exist. If we look around us at any given moment in a gathering of brothers and sisters, we will quickly discover that others have found different spokes in their quest to the Lord. When a person holds only to his or her "spoke" of faith without consideration for others, he or she falls into heresy or incomplete belief.

This is the reason God calls upon a diverse community to worship. One sister holds up her witness as a spiritual disciple; another brother offers the testimony of how God has led him to work with the poor. I am able to grasp God's completeness only through such sharing. What is it that the faithful are being called to hear from God through these people?

How can we create worship vehicles for the celebration of faith? What is the effect of the Good News for people at this time? Following are 15 models for creative calls to worship.

THE TRUMPET AND THE NAME

Dave and the students leading worship gathered outside the room to be used for the service. Two of the leaders stood at the door and made trumpet sounds with their mouths! I was amazed at how well the human mouth can re-create the sound of an instrument. (You also could substitute a kazoo for the mouth sounds.) The trumpets called each person to the doorway.

While this was going on, one of the leaders announced each person by his or her full name and led the worshiper to a seat. He did it in such a way so the person appeared to be a very honored guest at a royal reception. This was repeated until each member of the youth group had been personally called to worship.

TICKETS

One youth group used the call to worship as a way to invite other youth to the service. They mailed special tickets to each young person on the membership roll. The theme of the service was built around the book of Jonah. The tickets were designed to suggest that the holder could proceed to Nineveh. These passes were to be presented upon arrival at the meeting.

The room was decorated as if it were a ship. Sea sounds played in the background. The group members' participation in the call to worship was an opportunity to share why they had chosen to come to Nineveh when they could have gone somewhere else, like Tarshish. When the "passengers" were finally "on board," the next part of the service began.

FOOTPRINTS

Another youth group made 100 or more footprints out of cardboard. These prints were placed on the parking lot and on the floors leading to the worship area. The worship leaders met the worshipers as they got out of their cars. The worshipers were told that they could only enter by staying on the footprints. This created a line of people.

The footprints led beside a long route. At one point, the participants were told to move silently. At another place, they were asked to join hands. As they drew closer to the worship setting, the leaders told them to close their eyes and follow the person before them. This meant that they had to "feel" with their toes for a footprint.

When the people reached the room, the leaders asked them to keep their eyes closed as they were led to their seats.

FLOWERS

One youth group decided to use flowers to create the call to worship. The young people called the local funeral parlor and received huge floral arrangements left over from funerals. They found that there were several different kinds of flowers among the bouquets.

The worship leaders marked the seating sections with different flowers. As the youth groups entered the room for worship, each person was given a flower which corresponded with a certain seating section. The students were asked to walk in silence to the place marked by their particular flower.

This call to worship meant that a new community was created from the preformed groups who entered the room.

Later in the service, communion was served. As the students moved to the table, they were asked to place their flowers on the table and a new series of bouquets were created. These were later taken to shut-ins.

THE PUZZLE

A youth group launched a fall evening program by getting a blown-up photograph of their church. The 2-foot-by-3-foot photo was glued on a piece of Formica. Using a jigsaw, they cut this mounted picture into pieces. A small hole was drilled into each piece. The small, random-shaped pieces became part of a puzzle.

The youth mailed a puzzle piece to all the young people on the membership roster. Along with the puzzle piece, they sent a short notice that told the person that he or she was a vital part of their youth group. Each teenager was invited to bring his or her piece as the call to worship.

During the call to worship, each person came forward and contributed a piece to assemble the puzzle. The worshipers then focused on those who were present during the call to worship. Each person shared how he or she felt to be called as a part of God's puzzle.

At the end of the service, the pieces were randomly distributed with plastic string strung through the holes. Each person was asked to wear the puzzle piece during the next week and contact one of the persons who did not attend this service.

CIRCLES

A team of teenagers and I were conducting a retreat. The participants had come from many different places. How could I respect their uniqueness while moving them into community during a call to worship?

Using masking tape, we formed one circle on the floor for each person. We dimmed the lights and played a lonely pop song. One of the teenage worship leaders went out to the gathered group members. She told them to remain silent and then said, "Let us worship God."

We guided each worshiper to sit in a circle facing in different directions. The youth were now an organized group of separate strangers. The leaders asked the youth to close their eyes and reflect on what they had left behind. "What person's face do you most vividly see? What are this person's problems? What things have been left undone?"

The leaders moved the guided reflection into the present. They asked the youth to open their eyes and focus on a nearby person. The leaders guided the youth to think about that person's world, leave their circles and sit in pairs. They encouraged the pairs to share their earlier reflections.

After a few minutes, each pair found another pair. Their discussion led to the finding of another four persons. The call to worship continued in this manner until the new community had been created.

THE MAZE

One pastor and a team of college students were working on a worship for young people from many different places. Someone suggested that the call to worship was difficult because it seemed as if the worshipers were coming from so many different walks of life. This sparked the idea of creating a maze. By using boxes, masking tape, and turning off the lights in the hallways, the worship team members provided a journey each person had to undertake on the way to worship. Soft music and individual guides accompanied the people during this time.

MOTIONS TO WORSHIP

The youth group members were asked to wait outside the room where the worship was to be held. The youth leaders greeted each person with handshakes and hugs, not saying anything. They decided to use their bodies and motions to convey that the Spirit was calling this people to worship.

One of the leaders waved her hands in the air until everyone was looking at her. She put her finger to her lips to indicate silence. The worshipers then were encouraged to join hands as they were led into the dark room.

The chairs had been arranged in a large circle around an empty table.

The other leaders lighted two candles and placed an

open Bible on the altar. The three worship leaders used mime (simple hand and body movements) to show that the Holy Spirit was coming to the gathering.

THE ROPE

The youth retreat had been intense and moving. Forty young people had spent their time working and studying on a seminary campus. The concluding worship service was the climax of the community which had been created through work, prayer and sharing. The worship team of youth decided that Christ had linked them together. A long rope was chosen as the basic means of connecting the worshipers during the call to worship.

A member of the team asked the students to wander around the campus in silent meditation. After a few minutes, the leader of the team found one person and tied her wrist to the rope he already had tied to his. Then they went and found another person. They all embraced and tied this person's wrist to the rope. This was continued until the whole community had been connected and led to the place of worship.

WEATHER BALLOONS

I was a speaker at an exciting event for 1200 high school students. We had used four slide projectors, 16mm film, music and dialogue to draw us together. The four microphones in the aisles permitted a lively exchange; there had been laughter, debate and moving stories.

The planning committee of teenagers and I had struggled to create an appropriate call to worship. This invitation had to help us make the transition from a rich sharing time to a time of glorifying God as a community of faith. We decided to use the 10-foot weather balloons I had used earlier as screens. This was done by putting the slide projectors on the side away from the audience, and shining the image through the back of the balloons. This meant that the pictures could be seen on both the back and front of the balloons. (Weather balloons can be purchased at novelty stores or from Edmund Scientific, 101 E. Gloucester Pike, Barrington, NJ 08007. Toll-free 800-257-6173.)

For the call to worship, I loosened one of the weather

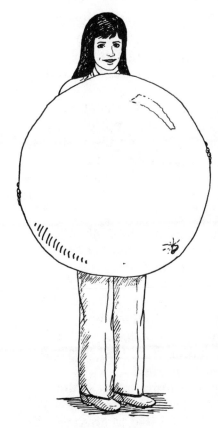

balloons from its mooring (a wastepaper basket) and held it in front of me. I then released the string which held the air in the balloon. Since there is very little pressure on the balloon, the air escapes very slowly.

I asked the students to think of the ways this balloon was like each of them. The students used the mikes and started sharing: "I get deflated by school and by the things others think I do wrong."

I gently pushed the balloon toward the students. I asked them to be gentle with it. Another girl shared her insight: "I am fragile and easily damaged by others."

As I continued this unusual call to worship, I asked the youth to share the ways the balloon was like Christ. Their moving comments were much more personal and revealing than the discussion we had had earlier. The transition to the rest of our worship was very easy.

TRUST WALK

The camp experience had been confusing, surprising and deeply satisfying. I had begun the day by gathering 200 strangers from several states into small groups. I informed them that they could use no language for the next two hours. As the evening worship time grew near, I wondered how we could move on from the day's experiences to the attitude of community worship. Fortunately, the camp provided an amazing call-to-worship opportunity.

The grounds bordered one of the most awesome spans of ocean beach I had ever seen. The dunes were huge; each step seemed to suck the foot into a bucket of loose sand.

After dinner, the youth leaders announced that we would prepare for the evening service with a call to worship which demanded our trust. We formed a long chain of interlocked arms and hands, closed our eyes and followed the person next to us.

We began a 40-minute call to worship. The deep sand, pounding sound of the surf and blazing stars kept us singing. God seemed to reach out and draw us into the vastness of creation. We ended on the edge of the water for the remainder of the service.

GOD'S MOSAIC

Bill and his youth enjoy hiking and camping at nearby parks. The youth in this church have found that very special worship moments have evolved on these trips.

One of the best calls to worship they discovered was what they called God's "mosaic." On one trek, the youth group stopped when they came to a point where worship seemed most fitting. Each person was asked to go out and find something which was an invitation from God for worship. After a few minutes, everyone returned.

Each young person had the opportunity to share the item symbolizing God's call to worship. After these insights were shared, the students were invited to arrange the items in the center of the worship in such a way that the mosaic showed the relationship between them. Bill reports that it was absolutely amazing how the items were woven into the perfect mosaic which proclaimed their call to worship.

OLD WOOD

We were conducting a series of worship services on Sunday evenings in Lent. The youth worship team was inspired by the cross as its biblical theme for the celebrations.

Their study of scripture revealed the role of wood as a continuing motif in the history of salvation; for example, the tree in Eden, Noah's ark, the Messiah image of a dry root, the cross.

Each week the youth used an old piece of wood as the call to worship. Since it was a small group, it was easy to involve everyone in the worship. The first week they gathered the high school students in a circle and placed the dirty piece of wood in the center.

The worship leaders asked each person to share the things which were ugly and unattractive about the wood. They then passed it around the circle and invited the worshipers to share the ways in which the wood symbolized something about their own lives. In only a few minutes, the people became a community of sharing; they were prepared to enter into worship together.

The piece of wood also was used at the end of the service. It was given to two worshipers, Joe and Betty, who were asked to "love" it in some way that would change the wood. It was to be returned for the next worship service. The following week, the wood was again used as the call to worship. "How has it become more beautiful because of the love Joe and Betty showed it?" The wood was cut into sections and given to each person at the end of the service as a symbol of the cross.

CLAY

The worship service was part of a Bible study with a small group of high school students. The teacher was a potter; she enjoyed the touch of shaping beauty with her hands. She and another student designed the calls to worship.

One week each person was given a piece of modeling clay. The teenagers were asked to close their eyes and think about difficult moments in the past week. After a while, the leader had the students focus on the happy times. She then played an upbeat Christian song and asked each person to shape a symbol of this happiness with the clay.

After a few minutes, the call to worship was celebrated by having each person show his or her clay sculpture and share the moment of happiness from the past week. They then formed a centerpiece with the clay symbols.

THE CEMETERY

Jon, a youth group president, was in charge of his youth group's Good Friday service. Jon also was a creative artist who loved to explore different art forms. He had experienced the simple art of gravestone rubbing in which you need tracing paper, tape and colored wax (crayons). The paper is taped across the face of the gravestone. When the wax is rubbed across the paper, the outlines of the images and words appear. Jon decided to use this art form as a part of the Good Friday service.

Jon led the youth group from the church to the cemetery. He gave each person the materials and asked the group members to prepare rubbings to symbolize Christ's suffering. They were asked to focus on the person the inscription was designed to memorialize.

After a few minutes, Jon led the youth back to a dark storeroom in the church. He reminded them that when they gather for worship, the whole church of Christ gathers through the Holy Spirit. For the call to worship, Jon invited the youth to show their gravestone rubbings and share the witness which might be given by the departed sister or brother. This was a way to acknowledge our forebears in the faith.

CHAPTER 5

Prayer Acts of Invocation

"Our Father, who art in ..." The Old and New Testaments and the Christian writers who followed left a vital legacy of words that focus on conversation with God. The Psalms, for example, touch each of us today as a way to express our happiness and pain before the presence of God. Church history has preserved a body of important written prayers.

Today's Christians continue to provide volumes of words to help us express our prayers. You probably have favorite books that play an important role in your prayer life. Written prayers are available in practically every style and form. In the chapters on prayer, I will not duplicate what others have already done.

There is a special role for the great written prayers of the church. You may come from a tradition that has been particularly faithful in preserving the prayers in your liturgy. Others may keep alive the words of prayer by reciting the Lord's Prayer or the Psalms each week in worship.

I am suggesting a different angle on the prayer element in youth worship. The word "act" best defines the concept of public worship. How can we enable the congregation to share their personal prayers as part of the corporate worship experience?

There are basically three styles of prayer in traditional public worship. First, there are *written* prayers which are read silently or recited (in unison or responsively with a leader). Second, there are *bidding* prayers which are offered spontaneously from people. Finally, there are *memorized* prayers which are spoken in unison.

I know that the recitation of memory prayers and the reading of printed words can be considered as congregational participation. I also recognize the importance of private, silent meditation when praying. Yet, the working theology of corporate worship used here demands that prayer should be the work of the people praising God. I am not sure that reading aloud in unison carries the same sense of belonging for contemporary youth that it once did. The purpose of designing prayers for creative worship is to facilitate personal involvement while maintaining a sense of congregational participation.

THE HOLY SPIRIT IN WORSHIP

I would like to share a few thoughts about my understanding of the role of the Holy Spirit in worship. My personal journey with the Spirit started in confusion and fear. I had been oppressed by people who flaunted their unique relationship with the Holy Spirit. In their sight, the only way I could be a Christian was to be exactly like them in my journey of faith.

I was also a bit gun shy about this part of my faith because I had the image in my mind of people rolling on the floor with foam coming out of their mouths. If this was the only way the Holy Spirit worked, I didn't want to let this aspect of faith enter my life.

I thank God for giving me some loving guidance concerning the Holy Spirit. Joseph Haroutunian, my mentor in theology at seminary, helped me discover (or be discovered by) the Holy Spirit through the Bible. I learned that the power of the Spirit was inseparable from my experience with Christ. In fact, the Holy Spirit in scripture is always present within the community of faith.

Biblically, people are always claimed by the Spirit in relationship to the body of Christ. For example, Acts reveals the Spirit touching and changing people with the agonizing imperative, "Arise up ..." These people are immediately bonded to their responsibility of being "Spirit" people. I suddenly realized that in giving my life to Christ and the kinship he created, I was responding to the work of the Holy Spirit.

There is mystery and power in how the Spirit works in my life. I have found that the source of my creative ideas is based on the working of the Holy Spirit. God touches and moves me continually in ways beyond my understanding and control. However, this lifestyle does not fall into the excesses which disturbed me during my youth. My understanding of the Holy Spirit is not based on exclusiveness nor strange behavior patterns.

This account of my understanding of the Holy Spirit is not meant to judge others who have a different experience. I merely stress the fact that the Holy Spirit is vital when approaching the invocation in worship. This understanding of the Spirit places this activity of God very close to you and your young people. The work of the Spirit will decide whether your creative service is a collection of gimmicks or an authentic moment of worshiping God.

THE ACT OF INVOCATION

There is something mysterious about invoking the name of God. The Bible records a continuous nervousness among believers concerning the name of God.

During his confrontation with God, Moses struggled to understand the name of the God who spoke to him out of the bush. Moses knew that if he could simply learn the name, he would be in control. God only revealed, "I am who I am" (Exodus 3:14). In the New Testament, people were healed through the use of Jesus' name.

I believe that the idea of God encountered in the veil of mystery does not give way to superstition. My use of the term "mystery" embraces a sense of the unexplainable, uncontrollable, uncontainable and untamable character of God. Anything I can say or understand about God, who is the focus of this worship experience, is always less than God. Jesus Christ has made the encounter between creature and creator both possible and necessary.

I will share 15 creative prayer acts of invocation. These

are meant to open your mind to ideas as you design this part of the service for your young people. We will begin with biblical phrases and let the prayer acts develop from them.

This practice of translating biblical teachings into acts of worship is one of the most important and helpful insights. It enables you to find new ideas while remaining faithful to the content of worship. You may want to paraphrase the favorite texts used in your tradition. All of the following biblical citations are my paraphrases. This will mean that you will not change the content of the prayer, but make it authentic through involving the worshipers.

PSALM 4:1

"Reveal yourself when I call your name, O God who vindicates me. You have expanded my world when I was in distress. Be kind to me and listen to my prayer."

The Psalmist calls upon the God who has already acted in his life. God has freed this person by making possible an appropriate way of acting or thinking. It is this sense of kindness and justice that serves as the basis for this type of invocation.

This text suggests an invocation that will enable your worshipers to call upon God's name. One high school youth group in Texas celebrated this insight by having the members form groups of two or three.

The leader then asked the youth to discuss and develop a statement which would complete a description of God's nature in terms of each person's life. In other words, how would they explain the nature of God as a result of their experience with the Lord? For example, each person was to complete the following sentence, "Reveal yourself to us as I call upon your name, O God, who _____."

The group reconvened and the service continued by having each person share his or her phrase of invocation. After each offering, the whole people responded by saying, "O Lord, be kind to us and listen to our prayers."

PSALM 18:1-2

"I feel tenderly toward you, O Lord, my strength.

*The Lord is my rock, my refuge and my deliverer.
My God, my rock, in whom I take cover; in whom
I will trust; my shield and the battering ram of my
salvation, my refuge."*

This affirmation of faith presents a belief that experiences the care and support of God. The writer utilizes the images of the rock and secures a place in describing how a relationship with the Lord can provide protection.

On a retreat, a New York youth group experienced this passage by gathering the worshipers in a circle. The Bible verses were read. A large rock was passed around and each person was invited to share the ways in which the rock suggested a worry or concern challenging his or her life.

The worship leader passed the rock around a second time. Each worshiper was asked to repeat the opening line, "I feel tenderly toward you, o Lord, my strength." Each person then had the opportunity to share how the rock symbolized God's comfort and security in the midst of troubles.

PSALM 27:7-9

*"Listen to my voice, O Lord, as I share aloud my
pain; be merciful to me and speak to me. You
have encouraged me, 'Seek my face.' My heart
says to you, 'Your face, O Lord, I look for.'
Please do not hide your face from me."*

The image of God's face suggests that compassion can be found in the Lord's presence.

A youth fellowship in Maryland gathered the worshipers in a circle. The worship leader posted the words of this passage, which he had copied before the service.

The verses were read aloud by the worshipers. Then the teenager leading the service passed a mirror to the others. Each youth was asked to look into his or her image and share the ways in which there was a need for God's favor (or face to be known). The worship leader encouraged the young people to make personal statements. The group was small and had become a community of faith. (The verses also could have been read in unison after each person commented on his or her reflection.)

PSALM 30:10

"Lend me your ear, O Lord, and look favorably upon me. O Lord, let yourself be the one who helps me."

A youth worship service utilized this verse. The leader encouraged the worshipers to hold hands and form a circle. Beginning at one end of the circle each person was asked to whisper in the ear of the person next to him or her. The focus of the comment was to be a reason why God's help was needed by this youth group. As each person did this, the whole group said in unison, "O Lord, let yourself be the one who helps us." After a person heard the private prayer of invocation, he or she squeezed the hand of the person who shared it.

PSALM 71:1

"O Lord, I flee to you; may I not be disappointed."

A youth fellowship in Australia used this verse for their prayer of invocation. The youth asked the worshipers to stand. The verse was read. The worship leader, Rich, told the people that they were going to invoke God by following the action suggested in the passage. The verse utilizes pursuing the Lord for security.

Rich asked the worshipers to start jogging in place. The active youth really entered into the spirit of this physical invocation. Rich passed around a towel. As each person took it, he or she was to share a moment of his or her life when it seemed tempting to run away from a problem or situation of shame. The verse was read between each sharing moment.

After the towel had been passed and each person had shared, the cloth was placed on the table as part of the worship centerpiece.

PSALM 77:2

"In the time of my trial, I search for the Lord: My hand reaches out continually, and my spirit cannot find comfort."

The Psalmist presents a picture of restlessness and need. There are times when everyone becomes restless and

impatient in the quest for God. We need to invoke the Lord
when this happens.

The youth worship leader, Jane, arranged the group so
that each worshiper was an arm's length from others. She
then had the youth close their eyes and raise their arms
straight out to their sides.

Jane slowly described a dark night: "You can feel the
restlessness of a hot summer evening ... There is something
on your mind which troubles you ... It is a trouble which
won't cease ..." This imaginary reflection on the troubles
facing the members of the group continued for two or three
minutes. Of course, the teenagers began to feel a discomfort
in their outstretched arms.

(Jane held her own arms out during this reflection.
This gave her a good sense of how uncomfortable the exercise was becoming.) The line from the Psalm was repeated.
Jane invited the worshipers to drop their arms and open
their eyes. They felt much better and were ready to encounter God's peace.

PSALM 82:8

*"Act now, O God, judge the earth; all the nations
belong to you."*

The youth adviser gave each person a page from a
news magazine. Each worshiper was asked to find something in the news which is offensive to God's love. Then,
each person was asked to share his or her example. This
invocation was particularly fitting because the previous
week there had been a terrible accident involving youth.
The invocation worked well in preparing for the forgiveness theme of the service.

PSALM 86:1

*"O Lord, give me your attention and respond to
me, for I am poor and I am needy."*

Sam, the president of the fellowship, read the verse.
He then organized the worshipers into four sections. Each
group was given a portion of the line ("O Lord, give me
your attention/and respond to me,/for I am poor/and I am
needy.") They practiced saying it in order. An offering
plate with a mirror was passed to each member in the

group. (Taped to the mirror was a small picture of a poor and needy person.)

Each person was asked to look into the plate and share a way in which he or she felt poor and in need of God's attention. When the person had stated his or her need for God's help, the rest of the group members responded with their four-part invocation.

PSALM 86:11

"Instruct me in your way, O Lord, in order that I may walk in all your teachings. Unbind my heart so that I may totally respect your name."

Jessie, the youth adviser, tied each person to a single length of rope. This was done by looping a section around one wrist of each person. The members were then asked to close their eyes and were instructed to move from the call to worship area to the center area. Jessie stopped them at various points to present one of the teachings of God. He used the Ten Commandments. (One or more of the Beatitudes also could have been utilized.)

When the participants arrived at the place for the rest of the worship experience, they were asked to sit down with the rope still joining them together. Jessie then read the verse which was posted on the wall.

Each person had an opportunity to share a teaching of God which had helped him or her the most during the last week. While each worshiper made his or her offering, Jessie had one of the youth worship leaders untie this person as the group repeated the invocation verse. This process continued until every hand (and heart) was untied.

PSALM 86:17

"Reveal to me an act of your love, so that those who hate me may understand their evil and be

put to shame. Lord, you are my helper and comforter."

Jan read the verse to the gathered worshipers. She encouraged them to close their eyes and focus on someone who had done something evil or unkind to them during the past week.

Jan helped the youth visualize this person by gently directing them to use their imaginations. How do the eyes look? What is the expression on this person's face? The participants were encouraged to relive the pain and hurt as they imagined the scene.

When the youth opened their eyes, a small wooden cross was passed around the group. Each person held the cross while the rest of the worshipers repeated the verse. Then the cross was passed on to the next person and the line was repeated.

PSALM 93:4

"More frightening than the crashing sound of floods, more frightening than the breakers of the sea, the Lord on high is even more awesome."

Laurie and the worship team secured a sound-effects album from the local library. They recorded several minutes of the sounds of floods and storms on a cassette tape.

The Sunday evening youth group was led into a darkened worship area as the sound was played. One of the students read the verse from Psalms. The worshipers felt the misty water which was being sprayed into the air by another student. (The youth used a plant sprayer to get the fine mist.)

Laurie passed a seashell around the group. Each person shared a time when he or she was frightened or awed by a flood, storm, ocean, etc. The verse was repeated after each person shared.

PSALM 104:24

"O Lord, how wide-ranging and complex is your creation. In your wisdom you have made every-thing; the world is full of your creatures."

When the people gathered in response to the call to

worship, Ernie, the worship leader, had the youth read the posted verse from Psalms. Ernie then passed around a puppy which he had brought along to the worship service.

He encouraged each person to hold the animal and share how God's creative miracle could be seen through such a small creature. The people repeated the invocational line after each contribution.

PSALM 139:1-2

"O Lord, you have searched me and known me! You understand me when I am sitting and when I am getting up; you grasp my thoughts from a distance."

Barry divided the worshipers into pairs and asked them to face each other. He then read the first sentence.

Encouraging the partners to closely look into each other's eyes, Barry suggested that they concentrate on the perspective of God's vision in that other person. What does God see in that other brother or sister? Barry reminded the worshipers to remain silent and make no comment. What are his or her needs? strengths? failures? The verse was read again.

Barry told the youth to face forward as he read verse 2. They then reflected on what God now saw within their hearts.

The worshipers then stood up as verse 2 was repeated. Barry asked them to reflect on what God sees about the activities in their lives.

Barry passed a marble around the circle and asked the people to imagine that this object represented the world from God's perspective. The youth were given the opportunity to share what they call upon God to see and understand about their lives. After this sharing, the two verses were read a last time.

PSALM 140:7

"O Lord, my God, my strong protector, you have covered my head during the time of danger."

Julie gathered the worshipers in a circle. She read the verse from Psalm 140. Each person was given a chance to share a moment in which he or she was in a dangerous situation.

Julie reread the verse and passed a large football helmet around the circle. Each person was encouraged to place it on his or her head. Julie then tapped each person's head. Each worshiper shared about the ways God protects him or her in times of danger.

PSALM 144:9

"I will sing a new song to you, O God; I will play to you on a 10-stringed harp ..."

Tom was a talented teenager. He immediately saw the possibilities of an invocation in this passage. After the people had gathered, Tom read the verse. Then he passed his guitar around the circle. He invited each person to pluck a string and share a bit of Good News as an invocation of God's presence.

The guitar was passed around once again. This time Tom showed each person how to make the sound of one note of a particular song. After each person had shared, Tom led the group in the singing of the new song.

CHAPTER 6

Prayer Acts of Confession and Pardon

Easy religion is very hot. Faith is always most popular when it tells us only how good we are. We like positive thinking, self-love, etc. Humans love to hear that they are wonderful. Although it is true that our relationship with Christ brings new life and worthiness, we are, by our nature, people who turn from God and thereby sin. We are tempted at every point to choose evil instead of good. Although we might not commit any "big" sin (e.g., murder, theft, etc.), we *are* sinful by nature. "If we say we have no sin, we deceive ourselves, and the truth is not in us" (1 John 1:8).

It is our acknowledgment of sin that enables us to embrace the saving love of God and to affirm ourselves. In every worship experience, people must have both the opportunity to feel the release from sin and the assurance of pardon through Christ. Authentic Christian worship cannot have one without the other.

We are accustomed to reading prayers of confession and pardon as a way of dealing with our sins before God in worship. This tradition presents a problem. On one hand, the words of confession come to us in beautiful forms.

They capture the spirit of sin. For instance, Psalm 51 provides a cry for God's forgiveness like no other. The theology of sin and forgiveness is clear.

Yet, we gather for worship with the emotional burden of countless sins. We need to be released. Jesus does not permit us to harbor "little sins" while feeling superior over those who commit "big sins." Those of us who turn from Jesus' love in our hearts are as sinful as those who act out their hatred on other people. Jesus is not compromising on this point. A careful reading of the Gospels always confronts the self-righteous person.

If sin is the burden of every believer, how do we tap into the reality of God's unconditional forgiveness in Jesus Christ? How can we *know* that we are new people after confession and pardon?

Many youth (and adults) in the church today seem hardly concerned about sin. The concept simply does not mean much to them. They may not have sinned against the standards of church, family or society. If they have, they may not feel much of a problem about sin.

Some experts are convinced that the young are turned away from God by a kind of "shame." They feel insignificant and unworthy because they have fallen short of their expectations for themselves. They haven't failed God in their thinking, but they have not lived up to the idealized view of themselves. The sin of pride is alive and well. Many people have made themselves the god which must be pleased.

What is the source of this kind of egocentric sin? Perhaps it rests in the kind of modeling we are forced to create in our society. There was a time when our mentors or models for development emerged from the close relationships we had with parents, grandparents and other significant persons. One important aspect of these relationships with the "saints" of our lives was that we could easily isolate the reality of their limitations and sins. They gave us a role model for certain attributes, but we were free to discover that they also failed.

But the modern world unfolds in such a way that our mentors are not present. Parents are often only seen briefly during some of the worse conditions. They become smaller than life. The models which are most frequently drawn to our attention are most often "bigger than life." The media project sports stars, film heroes and musicians in carefully crafted packages for optimum sales. Consequently, it is difficult to be comfortable with your own musicianship when all you hear are perfectly tailored albums. It makes no difference to our self-criticism that the particular album was remixed hundreds of times with all kinds of electronic enhancements.

The following prayer acts of confession and pardon need to be viewed from this perspective. We need to break through the walls that keep our youth from experiencing the full love and acceptance of Jesus Christ.

The book of James points us in the right direction. It suggests that we confess our sins to one another. I certainly understand this truth. When I sin against a member of my family, I know that God accepts my confession and forgives me. Yet, I personally need to confront members of my family and experience their affirmation of what God has already done in Jesus Christ. We need to know God's forgiveness through the affirmation of another. This is one reason why God calls us into the community of other believers.

The Catholic church has been particularly sensitive to human needs in relationship to sin by preserving personal confession and pardon. The world hungers for forgiveness. Since many Christians cannot experience the forgiveness of Christ in such a way that changes them, they deny that they have sinned. Young people are particularly battered by the world. They are told at every point that they are not up to standard (grades, acceptance by peers, adult criticism, etc.). Therefore, youth worship provides an exciting opportunity to deal with this vital aspect of our spiritual lives. Confession and pardon are preparation points in approaching the Word.

In a worship bulletin, you often may see that confession and pardon are separated. This may be necessary for the sake of informing people about the worship flow. However, please remember that confession and pardon are closely related. Design them as one act of worship.

I will share 15 prayer acts of confession and pardon.

These are meant to stimulate your thinking as your team designs this aspect of your service. Remember that some of the prayer acts may need quite a long time to complete.

SIN IS HEAVY

Confession. One youth group wanted to place the prayers of confession and pardon within the context of negative peer pressure. The team collected two baskets of medium-size stones to provide two for each person and a few more. As the worshipers began the prayers, they invited people to pick out two stones from the baskets.

The team members informed the congregation that the stones they held represented their sins. The leader asked the members to hold the stones out to their sides while Luke 17:1-2 was read. The leader mentioned that causing another to sin was like having the burden of a huge stone around your neck. If one is cast into the sea, he or she would drown under its weight. The stones were held out by the worshipers until they became very heavy and hard to hold up.

The worship leader then asked the members to lower their arms. He asked how their arms felt. The leader also asked the congregation to compare how the burden of holding the stones was like a life burdened with sin.

One person was selected from the congregation. He was asked to sit on the floor, hold a basket in each hand and stretch out his arms. The worshipers each were asked to place their stones in the two baskets at each side of the volunteer. The baskets also held extra stones. While the volunteer was struggling to hold them up, the other people took turns sharing how relieved they now felt without the strain of holding the stones.

The leader then asked the volunteer to share how he felt bearing the "sins" of others. He had mixed feelings of anger ("Why should I hold their stones?") and sadness ("It felt so lonely and unfair").

Pardon. The worship leader then asked each person to choose a stone from the baskets and express to the volunteer appreciation for bearing his or her burden. Each person went to the basket and took a stone. Some people thanked him with words while others hugged him.

The prayer act of pardon was completed by asking each person to exchange his or her stone with another person and say, "In the name of Jesus Christ, I assure you that God forgives you. Let me share your burden." The worshipers also agreed to pray for each other at noon each day for one week in order that the other person might be strengthened to resist sin.

SIN IS WAR

Confession. The youth group had been visited by a missionary who served in the Middle East. The members in charge of the next worship decided to deal with sin and war as part of their service.

They recorded sounds of war from a sound-effects record borrowed from the local library. They gathered the group of 25 around the worship center. The worship team played the tape of war sounds.

The youth worship leader read a brief newspaper account of the war and destruction which was going on in the Middle East. He passed around an unfolded handker-chief that was covered with dirt and mud so that everyone who handled it had dirty hands. The leader directed the worshipers to reflect on the symbols of destruction and death and think about the suffering they had heard about from the newspaper account.

Each person then had an opportunity to complete the phrase, "My sin is related to this situation because I ..."

Pardon. The worship leader read several Bible passages about the forgiveness promised in Jesus Christ. Then he went to each person with a clean, damp cloth and washed his or her hands. Another member of the worship team went behind the person being cleansed, touched his or her shoulders, and assured him or her of Christ's peace.

SIN IS PAIN

Confession. At one church, the youth discovered that they had a very special asset for their evening worship service—a very large, roughhewn cross. It was outside and lighted at night.

After the call to worship, Sue, a teenage leader, had the worshipers join hands and move outside to form a semicircle around the cross. She then passed an offering plate in which was piled small cut nails. These square-edged nails are very inexpensive and can be purchased at a hardware store. Each person was invited to take one.

The worship leader then asked the worshipers to clench the nails tightly in their palms. She read one of the Gospel accounts of the suffering of Jesus on the cross. Sue asked the worshipers to focus on the pain that Christ endured on the cross for the forgiveness of their sins.

After a couple minutes, the youth were asked to continue holding the nails and to think about a specific person upon whom they had inflicted pain and suffering. The leader guided them in using their imagination to picture the face of the oppressor and ask for forgiveness from this person.

Pardon. Sue asked each person to move to the cross and hammer the nail into it as a symbolic act of accepting God's forgiveness through the suffering and Resurrection of Jesus. Each blow of the hammer seemed to jolt the circle of worshipers. There were a few tears. The worshipers hugged each other in the joy of pardon and renewal.

SIN BURNS

Confession. The youth group was conducting a series of early-morning worship services on Wednesdays before school. One week they utilized an interesting means of confession and pardon. When the students came to the confession portion of the service, they were each given a book of paper matches. The worship leader read Psalm 51. He told them to remove one of the paper matches, separate the layers of paper and form a stick person. This figure was to be shaped to show the state of their feelings about their sin. A hymn was sung while the youth worked on their little stick persons.

The worshipers showed their stick people and shared their feelings about sin. They were not pressured to mention the particular sin.

Pardon. The youth placed their stick figures in an old metal bowl. The leader read a biblical promise of forgiveness. Then he burned the matches in the bowl. As the symbol of their sins burned, the group sang a hymn. (If you are planning on using this model, please be careful in picking a metal bowl. Fire is always dangerous and you will want to use a container that is totally safe.)

HIDDEN SIN

Confession. It was a very large youth gathering; but the adult and teenage leaders were struggling to keep it intimate and honest. They knew that it would be difficult to get the closeness which is so important to forgiveness.

When the students came into the worship area, they were given a brown bag. After the call to worship and invocation, they were asked to prepare for confession. The leader told them that sin is turning away from God's presence. In confession, we seek God's face. Yet, we are shameful of our failure.

The worshipers were then asked to put the bags over their heads as a way of hiding their sin from God. The leader then read Psalm 13:1-3.

Pardon. The worship leader offered the assurance of pardon ("... if you confess your sins, God will be faithful and just") and told them to take the bags off their heads. She asked them to put their hands around the mouths of the bags and blow them up. As an act of assured pardon by God, they broke the bags in unison. The joyous explosion of brown bags resounded throughout the hall.

SIN IS A PAIN IN THE SOUL

Confession. A youth leader stumbled upon a historical account of Christians in the Middle Ages who wore rough shirts under their robes. The coarse layer of material rubbed on the skin and was very uncomfortable. This practice was followed as a way to feel the price of sin.

The youth leader shared this practice with the worship team members. They felt that it would be good to help the teenagers experience the damage of sin in some physical way. It happened that they were going to leave soon on a group hiking trip. They decided to introduce the idea in that activity. After the call to worship and invocation, the members of the youth group were asked to stop along the trail. They were asked to remove one shoe. The worship leader asked them each to place a small stone in their shoe.

She explained that sins are sometimes very small. Yet, once we break the talking relationship with God, even the smallest breach brings painful experiences.

The students put their shoes back on with the stones in them. The group members then went back to their hike. They stopped when it became obvious that everyone had been feeling pain from walking on the stones. They went around the circle and each person shared a small sin which became a big problem in his or her life.

Pardon. The worship leader told the youth to remove their shoes and socks. She went around and knelt before each of the students. Using a scented lotion, she touched their feet and assured them that God in Jesus Christ forgives them of all sins.

SIN IN MOTION

Confession. The high school students had only 30 minutes to plan their section of the closing worship service at the youth conference. They had chosen to do the prayers of confession and pardon. There were 35 students in their planning group. Five minutes before the service, someone had an idea: "Doesn't all confession and forgiveness focus on Christ? Isn't Jesus on the cross the central issue?"

Another student had used mime at one time in her church. In just three or four minutes the team put together a confession and pardon prayer for the 700 students in the service.

When the time came for the prayers of confession and pardon, the 35 students marched down the aisle. Each person had assumed a role. The first two boys carried long poles (which they had found in a storage closet) as if they were spears. The boys moved and acted like soldiers. One person in the middle of the group was pushed and abused. He was obviously a prisoner. The rest of the parade people were the curious members of the crowd. But there was one other character, the beggar. He stumbled and limped as if he were physically and mentally unbalanced. He tried to join the crowd; however, they kept pushing him away.

The worship center had been prepared. It contained one chair. The crowd gathered around the chair. The soldiers "nailed" the prisoner to the "cross" by having him stand on the chair with his arms extended. The soldiers then used their spears to keep the crowd away from the crucified prisoner. The person on the cross "died." The crowd was silent and motionless.

Pardon. The beggar broke through the crowd and put the student playing Jesus over his shoulder. After the beggar had gently rested Jesus on the ground, he went up on the cross in the place of Jesus. A chill went through the congregation. You could hear people crying.

Then the person miming the role of Jesus got up and took the person down from the cross. The person waved his arms like he was flying away! Each of the teenagers in the group then went up on the chair and was released by Jesus and flew away into "heaven" (stage right). There was a touch of humor and joy in the final act of flying away. It was the perfect transition from the sadness of Jesus taking our sins upon himself to his love for us. Applause filled the room!

SIN IN PAIN

Confession. It was a Wednesday worship service during Easter week and the youth group was in charge. They wanted to create a service that would help the congregation experience the suffering of Christ on the cross. It seemed best to place this story at the point of the prayers of confession and pardon.

The youth wove together the Gospel accounts of the cross into a long narrative. When they came to confession, they asked the worshipers to enter into the passage and join Christ by lifting their arms out to their sides. The youth asked people to stand and spread out so that each person was not touching another person.

While the participants were holding their arms in this manner, the teenage leader had them close their eyes and imagine they were on one of the crosses next to Jesus. They were to focus on the burden and pain of their sins. Then, the leader slowly read the long narrative.

Pardon. The leader asked the worshipers to put their arms down. She reminded them that Christ forgave them through the act of the cross. In order to feel this gift, the leader had the worshipers form pairs. They took turns gently rubbing each other's shoulders so that they could experience the kinship of forgiveness in the community of faith.

SIN AND JESUS

Confession. A youth worker, George, was conducting the prayers in a youth service. He had been impressed by the small talk about a recent popular film which called on the imagination of the viewers. If the mind could entertain, why not use it in prayer?

It was a warm, summer evening. The windows were opened. At the time for the prayers of confession and pardon, George asked the youth to close their eyes and imagine that they were sitting alone in a room. Could they smell flowers? (He didn't suggest which kind of flowers.) They were asked to stand (in their imaginations) and walk to the door. Could they feel their hand on the knob? George continued to direct their imaginations on a walk outside the building onto a path. They were encouraged to feel the path beneath their feet.

George then asked the youth to look ahead, in their mind's eye, at a person coming down the path. The person looks familiar. He is smiling at them. It is Jesus! George encouraged the youth to look into the face of Jesus and see his eyes.

The leader invited the participants to feel Jesus putting his arms around them. Just feel how good it is to be close to him. George then suggested that they begin to feel a bit uncomfortable. They know that there are some things in their lives of which they are ashamed. They want to confess them to Jesus. The leader gave the youth a few moments to tell these things to Jesus in their imaginary encounter.

Pardon. George then guided the students into looking at the face of Jesus who slowly smiles. The youth are suddenly at the edge of the most beautiful body of water they have ever seen. George asked them to look at the color of it. Jesus asks them to step into the water. They can feel the perfect temperature against their skin. It is wonderful. They come out of the water and they feel so clean and pure.

George guided the youth back to the church building and the room where the worship was being held. When the students opened their eyes, there was an incredible spiritual power in the room. George asked the students to describe the kinds of feelings they had experienced in this prayer act of pardon. There was marvelous sharing from these young people. Many said that they had met Jesus for the first time!

SIN SEPARATES

Confession. The youth group was preparing a worship service and was trying to find a biblical passage that would help them communicate God's forgiveness. They focused on John 15:1-6.

At the proper point in the service, the worship leader asked the small youth gathering to stand and join hands. The leader read John 15:1-6 and asked the youth to imagine themselves as the living branches of God's vine.

The leader encouraged the youth to stretch their linkage as much as possible until they could barely hold on. He reread the passage while they continued to stretch. The pressure maintained because a couple members of the planning team were in the circle pulling at the human branches.

The leader asked the worshipers to think of a particular sin which pulls them away from God's vine. More pressure

was placed until the people couldn't hold on.

The leader then asked the participants to imagine that they were broken off and isolated from everyone. They were beyond all relationships: friends, family, church, school. He continued their imaginative separation by directing them to include other people who are broken off because of sin: the hungry, the imprisoned, the sick, the people trapped in chemical abuse, etc.

The worship leader passed a small bunch of grapes around the broken circle. He asked each person to share an example of how it feels to be cast away from God because of our fruitlessness or sin.

Pardon. The leader asked the youth to move closer and closer together until they could get no closer. He encouraged them to embrace one another as he reread the passages.

The leader passed around the grapes and asked each person to take one and eat it as assurance that God forgives and sustains the branches of his vine. The group sang "Bless Be the Tie" while this act of pardon was done.

SIN IS DELICIOUS

Confession. The students in charge of the worship service decided that confession and pardon must be seen in relationship to the Ten Commandments. When we break the covenant with God, we have turned from him. As the young people talked about the concept of sin, they picked up the image of the forbidden fruit in the garden of Eden. On newsprint, the youth copied the Ten Commandments. They posted this in the worship area.

When time came for dealing with sin in the Sunday evening worship service, they passed an apple around the circle. Each person was asked to select a commandment from the list. He or she was then asked to share how the apple symbolizes something about the nature of temptation to break this commandment. What made the forbidden fruit so appealing?

The apple was passed around the group once again. Each person was asked to focus privately on a particular way he or she had broken the commandment. The youth were asked to keep this confession private.

Pardon. The worship leader polished the apple and shared the promise of scripture that God is gracious and forgives us of all sin. He sliced the apple into sections and gave each person a piece. Each young person was invited to eat the apple to celebrate the fact that Christ comes to restore the covenant.

SIN IN CRISIS

Confession. The design team for the youth worship event decided to place the small group in a different seating configuration. They felt that the urgency of the Gospel would be experienced differently if they changed the setting of the service.

The team decided to worship in a crisis situation. How does our relationship to God alter when we face the end of our lives? How do we deal with the sin in our lives at this final time? The worship team members recorded the sounds of a plane in trouble from the sound-effects record they had borrowed from the local library. They arranged the chairs as if they were seats on an airplane. The chairs formed two rows with an aisle down the middle.

"Flight attendants" helped the worshipers to their seats in the call to worship. The darkened room featured only a few lights near certain points in the "cabin." They even used an intercom for the announcement of points in the service. The voice of the "captain" reported that they were taking off. The sound of the engine was played. In just a couple minutes the captain's voice told the youth that they were having engine trouble. Then the lights went out! Just before the prayer of confession, the captain said that she was sorry to inform them that they should prepare for a possible crash.

The "flight attendants" led the teenagers through a "bidding" style of prayer. This ancient form was used to encourage people to call out things on which the whole people should focus. After someone's voice lifted up a confession, the rest of the group was asked to say, "Forgive us, o Lord." The response was amazing. The heightened sense of crisis helped the students to bring their confession before God.

Pardon. There were a couple minutes of silence. The

group could only hear the groan of the recorded sound of an engine. The lights suddenly went back on. The flight attendant told the worshipers that all was now well with the plane. A male and female worship leader went down the aisles as flight attendants. They asked each person to extend his or her hands. Both hands were wiped with a wet cloth. The leaders looked each person in the eye and said, "In the name of Jesus, I assure you that you are saved from all sin."

The rest of the service focused on the students' reaction to this dramatized danger. A wonderful service!

SIN AND SOAP

Confession. The confirmation class had scheduled regular worship services as part of their preparation for public confession of faith. One week, the worship team wanted to focus on the confession and pardon, which they had been studying.

They read Psalm 51. The leader then passed around a bar of soap. Each person was asked to share the good memories he or she had about a bath or other time he or she used soap. "What was the time when you were most pleased to wash your hands?"

The teenager who was leading this part of the service passed the soap around once again and asked each person to focus on some sinful part of his or her life.

Pardon. The worship leader read the Psalm once again. Then she went around and gave each person a small, wrapped bar of soap. As she handed it to each one of the students, she assured them that Jesus forgave all of their sins. The students were given an opportunity to share how it felt to have a pure heart.

SIN AS ICE

Confession. I was with young people from many different churches in the area. The 150 teenagers were concluding a weekend winter retreat. This was going to be the end of our time together. We had played in the snow, warmed ourselves by the giant fireplace, sung hymns, studied the Bible, worshiped and talked late into the night.

Our team came up with a delightful idea for confession

and pardon. We had been discussing how the temptations of sin are so temporary and yet they cause such long-term damage in our relationships with God and others. Finally the ideas all came together.

When we came to the time of confession, the teenager who was leading worship read Psalm 51:1-6. Randy then told us that we would be singing for the next few minutes as we focused on our sins. He read James 5:15.

The worship leader pointed to three circles made of masking tape in the center of the worship area. The circles were big enough for four or five people to stand in if they were huddled together. These were the circles of confession. If anyone wanted to come forth in the course of the singing and put to rest the burden of sin, he or she could join the two people (a counselor and teenager) in the circle. They were asked to pray with the individuals when they came to confess.

Pardon. When we had completed this process, we moved into the act of pardon. Randy presented us with three large snowballs then read Psalm 51:7. He passed the icy balls around the group and asked each person to wash his or her hands. Towels were carried by the adults to dry the hands of the worshipers and personally affirm them of the forgiving act of God in Jesus Christ.

POLLUTION IS SIN

Confession. The youth group had done several programs on creation. The young people had been taught that Genesis 1 suggests that God responded to his creation with the affirmation, "and God saw that it was beautiful." The word "good" had been replaced by a word which implies that we are called to be artists in care of the world.

The worship service included an interesting prayer act of confession and pardon. In the center of the worship circle, the youth had placed a globe. Each person was invited to choose something from a basket of pollutants: bug spray can, oil can, empty soft drink container, paper, etc.

Each person was then invited to take a turn and go to the globe and pollute it! The leader read selections from Genesis 1. Each worshiper was given a chance to describe how the pollutant was doing something harmful to the earth. Each person then shared how he or she contributed to the sin of defiling God's creation.

Pardon. The leader removed all the pollution symbols from the globe and reread the passage. She then gave the students a small, clear glass marble and asked them to accept their forgiveness by carrying the marble with them during the next week. They were asked to share the joy of their pardon by intentionally doing something every day to clean up the earth.

CHAPTER 7

Prayer Acts of Intercession

It is easy. It is proper. We do it without thinking. In fact, reaching out on behalf of another is the very foundation of Christian love. Christ's love for us is most apparent through the prayer acts of his own life. The prayer of forgiveness and the acts of love from the cross reflected his whole ministry.

One of the more difficult aspects of caring for others is making sure that pity is not substituted for Christian love. Christian concern is not rooted in the reduction of others for the sake of our own superiority. There are no one-sided acts of intercession. We receive from others as we serve them.

The epoch passage in Acts 9:10-19 clearly illustrates the process of intercession. As you recall, Paul had been physically blinded by his revelation from God on the road to Damascus. Ananias, a Christian, is suddenly given the role of God's intercessory agent to help Paul. But Ananias is blinded by his limited view of God's power. Ananias can only see Paul through the perspective of his worldly criticism. He initially refuses to obey the Spirit in helping Paul. God compels the two men to serve each other. Ananias is God's agent to heal Paul's physical blindness while Paul is God's agent to heal Ananias' spiritual blindness. They *exchange* acts of intercession.

This passage teaches us that we must reach out to those in need in order to complete our relationship with God. The poor, the oppressed, the outcast and the sick all have something to give us as we serve them. True compassion stems from respect and appreciation for God's creatures. If we pity or look down upon those in need, we pity the Creator who made them. God is not to be pitied! We are serving Jesus in our intercessory acts toward another. Our Lord becomes the sick, the hungry, the dying and the oppressed. Those in need have thus been uplifted and dignified by Christ.

We have often been puzzled why people reject the Gospel. Perhaps one reason is that the Good News has been transmitted by "better-than-thou" Christians who say they will "pray" for people, but do nothing to help them. The Gospel has been cheapened by this degrading presentation of Christ.

Our approach to prayer acts of intercession must be looked at in the context of the work of the Holy Spirit in the Christian life. God has forged an eternal community in the work of Christ which transcends every human condition. When another person twists in pain or sobs in loneliness, the whole body of Christ aches. Every part of the body is connected to another. We draw upon this kinship in our prayer acts of intercession.

This understanding is not the way of the world. Every appeal for funds is based on a picture of a starving person. I am pleased that this kind of advertising brings a response of generosity; however, the Christian prays out of a different kind of compassion.

A friend who faces life from a wheelchair tells me that such a secular condescending approach to getting help for the handicapped is often a disservice. The poster approach results in attitudes of sympathy from people who can only see my friend's wheelchair. They can't imagine that they are standing before a capable woman with two master's degrees. Christians are often the most guilty of this kind of pity reaction. This is a good reason for the creative and experiential approach to prayers of intercession in youth worship.

There is another vital opportunity at this point in the

service. There should be a direct relationship between praying with our minds and actually responding to the needs of others. As Jesus prayed for our forgiveness from the cross, he forgave us with his pain, suffering and death. Words and action are inseparable in biblical faith.

Prayer and life are simply different sides of the same coin. This means that worship will need to create opportunities for faith and life to meet. Many youth groups have found that intercessory prayer acts are often excellent places for sending people out to serve. We have the freedom to place this aspect of the worship experience at the end of the service!

I will provide 15 examples of creative prayer acts of intercession. These come from specific times and places. You may have to adjust an idea for the size, setting and time frame of your particular worship event.

BENDING TO THE NEEDS OF OTHERS

Ann, one of the youth group members, had just spent a few days in the hospital for the setting of a broken bone. She had been in a ward where others were seriously injured in car accidents. Many of them would never walk again. As Ann shared her story, others on the worship team were struck with an idea to bring people into an intercessory act.

At the time for this prayer in the service, the leaders passed offering plates filled with inexpensive paper clips.

The worship leader asked each person to take a paper clip. She read a section from Isaiah 53 which tells how the suffering servant will be rejected and abused. The leader then asked each person to focus on someone in need. While the youth were reflecting on the needs of this person, they were urged to reshape the paper clip to symbolize the needs of others.

After a few minutes the youth passed the plates again and collected the wire sculptures. One youth led a prayer for the needs represented in the offering plates. The paper clips were then passed again. Everyone was urged to take one as a symbol of carrying the burden of another person from this place of worship.

The worship leader asked the teenagers to carry the

paper clips each day during the next week. The leader urged everyone to find one person every day who needed an act of care and love. The youth were to serve this person. The young people were asked to bring back the bent wire to the next worship and share how it had changed in meaning (and perhaps shape) through the acts of service to others.

INTERCESSION AS A FREE GIFT

The youth group had been promised the opportunity to do something special for the Advent season. On the Sunday before Christmas, Bill, the president of the youth group, was given the opportunity to do the prayers of intercession.

He told the congregation that we are called to pray for others and to back up prayers with action. Since it was the Christmas season, giving and receiving was on most everyone's mind. Bill said that the youth group wanted to give the congregation a worship experience in which they would serve as well as receive.

The youth group had polished beautiful apples, wrapped them in foil, and placed them in huge baskets at the doors of the church building. Bill said that the youth group would give each person an apple at the door on the way home.

The congregation's special intercessory charge for the next week was to give the apple to someone they did not know. They were encouraged to tell the person that the apple was given because of God's great gift in Jesus Christ. They would complete this intercessory act by sharing their stories during the following Sunday's worship service. As each person was given an apple at the door, the youth group members said, "May the peace of God be with you on your mission."

The following Sunday, when it came time for the prayers of intercession, it seemed that just about everyone had a wonderful story of witness and sharing. The lonely, lost and angry people the worshipers met gave them great gifts of love in return. Several people confessed that they kept putting off giving the apple to another person because of fear.

One woman prayed with a sick lady in a stranger's house. A group of teenagers approached a group of toughs and were shocked to see their appreciation when the rough teenagers learned about the intercessory charge. The toughs had received only suspicion and anger from other people. The stories again and again showed how much people in need had given to the Christians who had reached out to them.

The long sharing time in the service was concluded by the distribution of apple wedges. The people were encouraged to take a piece, eat it, and remember that God calls us to care for others by our prayers and acts. The words of the concluding prayer focused on the people who had been encountered by this outreach. What a marvelous way to combine prayer and action on behalf of others.

VOICES OF INTERCESSION

Sometimes prayers of intercession can come from unexpected places. I was leading a workshop in Kansas City. Part of my work was to help youth become equipped to do ministry. After spending the opening hours in Bible study and building community, I taught them the basics about interviewing and how to use a simple cassette tape recorder. We then went outside into the area to capture the stories of others.

We went to a nearby retirement home and visited many different rooms in teams of two. I was delighted to see what the youth could do. They had come across some of the residents who were from their church. These sensitive and clever teenagers then had these elderly members record short prayers.

When we returned to listen to our tapes, we were all struck by what these elderly people had said. Their prayers were not for themselves, but rather they were praying for the people in the church!

The pastor suggested that we use these taped prayers in the Sunday morning worship service. The time for the prayers of intercession came. The pastor told the congregation that they would now receive prayers from those who were part of the body, but who were not present. After he played the tapes, there wasn't a dry eye in the church.

Here were people who were in pain, lonely and close to death; yet they reached out and prayed for others.

As a result of this youth group ministry in the intercessory prayer act, a number of adults in the church visited their relatives and friends who had been neglected in the retirement home.

THE INTERCESSORY PHONE

One church I know values mission outreach. The members have supported youth involvement in workcamp situations. The people also are aware that others doing ministry need intercessory support during times of actual service.

The pastor worked out a system so that the whole congregation could hear a phone conversation. (Each area and phone system are different; however, electric supply stores, phone companies and even church members can rig such a system for you.)

The young people who were at a workcamp called the congregation during the worship service. The minister was flexible with the order of worship and found that it was quite easy to plan the intercessory prayer at the time of the call.

The young people reported to the congregation about their work and the prayer needs of the people being served. The congregation then prayed for the young people and their work. The impact on both the youth and the congregation was visible and powerful.

The congregation uses this system to talk with missionaries all over the world. This adds an immediacy to our prayers for others far away. It also is nurturing and sustaining for those who must serve alone in other places.

BETWEEN A ROCK AND A HARD PLACE

The youth group had a program on teenage suicide. There had been a recent suicide of a local high school young person. As the youth talked about loneliness and the other factors which put pressure on teenagers in the community, they realized that they needed to do intercessional prayer work among themselves.

The next Sunday the youth adviser, Betty, led the worship service. Betty gathered the 20 members in a large circle. They went through the usual facets of their worship service; however, she focused on intercessional prayer. "Do we really pray for each other? How do we pray for each other?" she asked.

Betty had piled a selection of 50 or 60 small stones in the center of the circle. She read Psalm 62, focusing on verses 2 and 6, "He only is my rock and my salvation ..."

Then she asked each person to pick a rock which best reflects these verses. How can God's protection be seen, in some way, through a particular stone?

After the worshipers had each chosen a stone, Betty had each person share a few phrases to indicate how this stone reminded him or her of God's support. This sharing of intercession went on a long while. People really opened up about how they needed others.

Betty asked the youth to form pairs with the person next to them. They were to exchange stones and talk about particular needs in their lives at that moment and the next week.

Betty had the students form an intercessional prayer covenant for the next week. The youth agreed to carry the other person's stone and pray for him or her at the same time each day. Each pair chose its own time for this intentional intercessional prayer. At the next worship service the worshipers shared their feelings about praying for another person as he or she prayed for them.

INTERCESSORY HEALING

The 150 youth in the Portland area enjoyed the spring retreat in the mountains. Just before we were to return, the area was struck with a freak snowstorm; the power went out and the buses couldn't get through. None of us were worried; yet, we had exhausted our food supply and we had several hours to wait.

The focus of the retreat had been the power of God in our lives. We decided to continue our program even though it was scheduled to be over. Someone asked me about the miracle stories we had briefly explored in the course of presenting the theme.

Another student mentioned that a beloved youth

worker, Max, was critically ill with cancer. It suddenly hit us that we should pray for this person. God was nudging us to draw upon his power instead of talk about it.

I asked the teenagers how we should go about focusing our prayer energy for Max. One person suggested that we learn exactly what was wrong with him.

I posted newsprint and asked some of the people who were close to Max to share the specific nature of his illness. A nurse was able to draw the part of the body which was being attacked. She also described how the body needed to fight the cancer.

A young person thought we needed to gather closer together so that our faith would have more energy. We held hands in a large circle. Another person started singing and we all joined in. The words and phrases for Max were highly directed. The young people poured their hearts out to God on his behalf. There were tears and a strange sense of peace and strength in that group. The prayers went on for 45 minutes. The buses finally arrived. With the state police leading us, we headed through the mountain passes and made it home. The good news on our arrival at the church was that Max had made it through his immediate crisis. A cheer went up from the group. You couldn't convince us that God hadn't been with us as we reached out on behalf of this brother.

I talked with Max a couple years after this incredible prayer act of intercession. He is convinced that the prayers of this loving youth group carried him through.

MOST WANTED

A youth group in Detroit was having trouble planning the intercessional prayer for the Sunday evening gathering. They found it quite easy to pray for those who were sick, poor or in need; however, the planning team found difficulty with the idea of praying for "bad" people. "Bad" people were defined as those who had never done anything to them directly, but were evil or living a non-Christian life.

Ray, the youth adviser, listened and then suggested that the "bad" people were the ones who needed the most prayer. His rule of thumb is to focus *only* on the issues or

problems with which the youth have the most trouble dealing. Ray believes that these sensitive areas are the most
open for the impact of the Gospel. He operates very differently from those who program by trying to avoid anything which might unsettle or confuse.

One of Ray's students
mentioned the "wanted"
posters which he had seen
in post offices as a symbol
of "bad" people. That comment triggered an idea for
the prayer act of intercession.

When the service came
to the point of praying for
others, the worshipers were
given individual copies of
several "wanted" posters.
They were asked to read
the brief descriptions and
look at the photograph as if
the young person were the
parent of this fugitive. How
could you plead a case for
this person before the
throne of God? Was he or
she the victim of poverty or violent family life? A member
played a Gospel hymn about sin on a guitar while the
group reflected on this person who needed their prayers.

The 20 worshipers shared their stories on behalf of the
fugitive they represented. It was hard going. Finally, the
worship leader reminded the participants of Jesus hanging
on the cross between two criminals. He asked them to
share a "circle" intercessional prayer. This was done by
each person adding a sentence or two of a prayer for these
fugitives. They went around the room again and prayed for
the victims of the crimes allegedly committed by the people in the posters.

HUNGER

A youth group in Spokane was impressed by the program on hunger. The speaker drew them into the wide-spread problem which existed not only in the Third World, but also in their own city.

The youth designed a lock-in (18 hours in their church building) to study this basic human concern. If Christ promises that we feed him when we feed the hungry, aren't we committed to be involved directly? The youth council wanted to create an event which would be more than just a time to feel sorry for others. It became clear that they would have to take their members through the actual experience of hunger in order to make the spirit of inter-cessional prayer and service more than an act of charity.

The retreat began at 5 p.m. The youth group members were told not to eat anything after lunch. This super event focused on their personal hunger, the extent of the problem in the world and how they can do something about it.

The intercessional prayer followed the study of the extent of world hunger. The young people had just seen a documentary film on hunger across the world. At this point (early evening), the youth were getting hungry themselves.

A large picture of a starving child was posted in the front of the worship group. A mirror was passed around the prayer circle and each person was asked to study his or her face. How would prolonged hunger change the way they looked? The planning team had recorded the sound of a heartbeat from a sound-effects record borrowed from the public library.

Then each person had a chance to share what particu-lar gift God could give the starving person. What is needed to keep going?

Around midnight, the youth gathered for worship again and offered prayer acts of thanksgiving as they tasted bread, their first food.

Before the group members left the next day, they went back to intercessional prayer and committed themselves to do a specific thing to work on the hunger problem. Some amazing service projects came out of this lock-in. During the Sunday morning service, the young people were able to share the results of their time together. They told the con-gregation of their hunger experience and also outlined what they were going to do about hunger.

THE MENTOR

In the preparation of the worship service, a group of teenagers started talking about the best teachers they ever had. The youth adviser suggested that they pick up this theme in their intercessional prayer acts. The idea of the "mentor" or guide emerged. Which people had helped the youth to learn? Which people had given them opportunities to participate? Which people had given them emotional affirmation?

During the intercession, the worship leader read Deuteronomy 6:4-7 as a model of a mentor (teaching in all of your life, walking, sitting, lying down, etc.).

The worshipers passed around a large coffee can containing many crayons. Each person was asked to choose a crayon which symbolized the person who most influenced his or her life.

The worshipers shared their reflections on the most influential person in their lives. The leader reread the text and asked the worshipers to reflect on the needs of the person who gave so much to their lives. In what ways does this person need God's love?

The leader then passed out paper and pens. Each person was asked to write his or her mentor a note which expressed his or her feelings about the gift received. These notes were collected and (if possible) mailed to the mentor.

SHADOWS OF NEED

One evening the youth group in Nashville decided to have its Sunday evening worship service in a dark storage room. They were focusing on the theme of light in the New Testament.

During the prayer acts of intercession, the youth focused on the needs of others by using light and darkness. They arranged a single light so that it was easy to create shadows.

Each person was encouraged to silently reflect on a particular person who especially needed God's love at this time. A recording of a hymn was played during this time of silent meditation.

The teenage worship leader then asked each person to make a shadow figure with his or her hands to symbolize the person or the person's need. There was some laughter at first; yet, the youth leader encouraged the students to talk about the person for whom they were praying.

The leader then placed a cross between the light source and the hall. In the shadow of the cross the worshipers finished their prayers of intercession.

IN THE NEWS

The youth officers noted that their group members were woefully unaware of the world. The young people's concerns seemed to focus on the life in their community. Their attitude was "The world can take care of itself."

The officers designed a portable service in which the youth would literally move through several different rooms in the course of the worship experience.

During the prayer acts of intercession, the worship leaders led the group into a large room and lined the students around the border of a large newspaper. The leaders had created this mega-newspaper by taping together the edges of full sheets of newspaper. They found that it was important to tape both sides for this massive newspaper. The outside edges were also taped so that it wouldn't rip.

The worshipers were asked to step forward, lift the paper and walk under it. The group members were able to create a tent-like paper over them.

The worship leader read John 3:16. He stressed that God so loved "the world" that he gave his only Son. "The world" was defined as every possible place and every possible life setting.

The leader then asked certain people to step back from under the huge newspaper tent. As each person left, the part which he or she had been holding began to sag. Soon, the few remaining people were almost buried by newspaper. The leader asked the few people how it felt to hold up the giant newspaper. Of course, they complained that it was impossible without more help.

All of the students were then invited to return to the outside edge of the newspaper. The worship leader asked them to remove their shoes.

The leader reread the passage and explained that the

whole creation needs to be sustained by the prayers of all. He invited the youth to walk carefully to a spot on the huge newspaper and sit down. The worship leader explained that the prayers for others need to be focused.

A hymn was played as the students searched the piece of newspaper around them for stories of people who needed their prayers. These were then shared. The whole group recited John 3:16 between each prayer for intercession.

INTERCESSIONAL CARTOONS

The youth planning team of a church in Akron realized that humor was an important ingredient to their special mix of people in the youth group. Yet, when they came to worship, it always seemed so deadly dull. Why not use humor in worship? God has a fine sense of laughter; it is one of his greatest gifts to us.

The planning team decided to draw upon this resource for the intercessional prayer act. The team members collected the most popular newspaper comic strips. Using white paper, they covered the words in the "balloons." that contained the dialogue.

During the prayer of intercession, the leaders distributed the comics and pencils. They asked the youth to reflect on someone they knew who had particular needs. "If God were speaking through the comic you are holding, what would be written in the dialogue balloons?"

The ideas were shared. There was laughter; however, it was amazing how moving some of the stories and responses were from the worshipers. The leaders closed the intercessional act with a prayer circle focusing on the concerns of others.

PARENTS

A Canadian youth group had been studying the nature of the Christian family on a retreat. They had probed how a mature child has the ability to understand the pain and needs of his or her parents. The immature child only thinks of himself or herself. Such an immature person merely reacts to parents.

The youth wanted to incorporate this insight in the

closing worship experience. The worship leader read
1 Corinthians 13. She used the Revised Standard Version,
which used the phrase, "in a mirror dimly" in verse 12.

The worship leader passed a large soup spoon around
the circle and asked each person to look at his or her image
reflected in the spoon. Each person appeared upside down
and very dimly. It was truly "in a mirror dimly." Each person was asked to share one thing his or her parents think is
childish ("thought like a child") about their child's outlook
and behavior.

Then the youth were asked to turn the spoons to the
other side. Their image now appeared right-side-up. The
final verses of the passage were reread. Each person had an
opportunity to share how the adult perspective, shaped by
love, can enable him or her to see a need of his or her
parents.

The final intercessional prayer act was to make a verbal
commitment to help parents in a specific way during the
next week. These experiences were shared at the next
regular youth group meeting.

NATURE

The youth group was on a camping trip. The main part
of the weekend was spent hiking. The group found that
such a setting is fantastic for worship.

The young people were using Genesis 1 as the biblical
theme for their outing. It was clear from their study that
God had entrusted the creation to us. What kinds of
stewards are we of Earth?

The prayer of intercession was held at a campsite
where previous campers had failed to clean up the area.
The youth adviser had a sudden inspiration. He read
Genesis 1 and asked each person to begin the prayer act of
intercession by going out silently into the nearby area and
finding something about nature that particularly needed the
youth group's prayers. The young people were to bring
back a symbol of this need.

In a few minutes, the youth returned for the prayer act
of intercession. Each person shared items which he or she
had found about fragile nature. One teenager produced a
pair of broken sunglasses. "I offer my prayer for the human

creatures who can't care for the earth." The group members concluded their prayer act by cleaning the area as best they could.

AIRPORT NEED

A youth group in a rural mining town focused their time together by taking "mystery" journeys each week. The van full of youth (usually five to seven) would go to a different place each week in order to perform a ministry and worship God in a fresh environment.

One week they went to a major airport and gathered in a snack area. The adviser told the youth that this was their living prayer of intercession. During this active prayer they were to relate to a stranger. Once the person's needs were understood, it was their task to pray for this person by helping him or her. They then canvassed the airport in pairs.

The young people had some amazing experiences. One pair met a young woman with three children. Their flight had been delayed and her youngsters were fussy. The two youth befriended them and calmed the children and mother.

One pair came across a woman who had spent the night at the airport. Her father had died and she was struggling with her feelings of guilt. She hadn't seen him for a long time and had a bad relationship with him.

When the pairs gathered for formal prayer, the young people focused on the people they had met. They asked for God's blessing and help for these specific people's needs.

CHAPTER 8

Prayer Acts of Petition

Jesus did it. Paul did it. Why can't we? I am talking about praying for ourselves. It is obvious from the Bible that God permits the believer to ask for help in his name. Yet there are those who don't think that it is proper to pray for one's self.

Prayer is the focus of our continuous conversation with God. It is not selfish to bring everything to God in prayer. I believe that it is proper to ask God for miracles in our lives. It is true that we must follow the example of Christ in the garden by combining our direct request with the act of finally submitting to God's will.

As a former hospital chaplain, I have experienced too many results from prayer in life and death situations to take this aspect of prayer lightly. God *does* listen to us in prayer.

It is also important to struggle with the place of God's will in our lives. I have found that I am living under the lordship of God; he is directing my life. I have not always appreciated his will in decisions. In fact, I find that God speaks to me continually through many "burning bushes." The difficult part of seeking God's will is listening. I have missed his direction when I have failed to respond to his beckoning through other people and my intuition. If Christ is in us, we can trust that small, internal voice that speaks to us.

It is unfair for us to label a crisis in someone else's life as God's will. A time will come when that person will look back and see how God was speaking at that time. However, it is up to him or her to make this discovery. We are to be ears of understanding for hurting brothers and sisters. We are not to be pointing fingers of God's judgment.

Such an understanding helps youth when they share everything with God in prayer. The young have many difficult decisions to make in an ominous world. The old perceptions of vocation, love relationships, science, government and security have all changed. Things will never be the same as before in terms of cultural patterns. However, the Christ we serve is more meaningful than cultural, economic and social traditions; he is seen in the forms we follow. He is Lord of all time and life. We tend to present a small God in a specific time frame to our youth, but we must transcend our culture and search for the genuine Christian response.

There is something wonderful about praying for one's self in public worship. The act pulls an isolated person into the healing realm of the community! There is an intercessory dimension to the prayer of petition because a person is actually praying as part of the whole community of God.

These theological reminders are important in helping the young person face a talking relationship with God. He or she needs to know the God who can both touch an individual and create and sustain the cosmos. The sense of immediacy and presence lies next to the awareness that God is Lord of all; a miraculous encounter for all of us.

I am sharing 15 prayer acts of petition. We are servants who are trying to provide the opportunity by which God can speak to the deepest personal needs of our youth.

PETITION FOR HEALING

The youth group had been doing an extensive Bible study. They had been intrigued and puzzled by the accounts of healing by Jesus and his disciples. This particular church had no experience with direct healing.

The youth leader, Steve, talked with the pastor about

this topic. They were not comfortable with the healing style which came across on some of those television evangelists' shows. Yet, the two did believe that God's healing prayer was powerful. Jesus does heal!

For one of their worship services the pastor and the youth adviser worked with a group of teenagers on healing. They studied James 5:13-16. A note was sent to the parents explaining the special nature of this service.

The people gathered and worshiped God. During the prayer of petition, the leaders explained that God has healing power to cure us of all afflictions. Yet, such healing is not a magic show, as God works in many ways to answer prayer.

Steve asked for people to share the ways God works in healing today. Some suggested that this power was seen through the healing work of doctors and nurses. Another mentioned the wonder of science in saving his prematurely born cousin. "This would have been impossible just a few years ago," he said.

The worship team passed around index cards and pens. Each person was asked to name a particular aspect of his or her own life which needed healing by Jesus. The names of the persons were to be omitted. The cards were then folded and collected.

Steve read each of the cards and paused for a word of prayer. The youth were encouraged to add a word or phrase in this prayer circle; many thoughtful prayers were offered. The group was led in a requested prayer for the needs of the members.

Steve then held up a bottle of cooking oil. He told the group that this was simply the regular grocery store product. Steve poured some of the oil into a shallow silver bowl and read James 5:16.

Steve said that he would move around the circle and would anoint anyone on the back of the hand who wanted to experience the words from the prayers of petition. The response to this service was excellent. This youth group now includes the anointing prayer at least twice a year. Furthermore, there were others in the congregation who wanted to attend the next service.

It is important to note the sensitivity with which the

youth leadership handled this mode of prayer. Every idea in this book is practical for each situation that comes up if we are caring and sensitive to our people. In the hands of less capable youth and adults, this service could have caused some misunderstanding.

LONELINESS

The youth group was small, yet their worship time was important. They had developed a lot of trust over the past eight months. One of the themes emerging from their discussions and informal conversations was the sense of personal loneliness many of these youth were facing.

One winter evening, they creatively addressed this need during the petition part of the service. Everyone was served a cup of hot chocolate. The worship leader shared several stories from the New Testament where the forebears of our faith were lonely and isolated, Jesus in the garden, Peter after the arrest of Jesus, and Paul during his ministry. Steve made the point that loneliness is a painful and natural human state.

For the prayer act of petition, Steve asked each person to examine the small piece of wood he or she had been using to stir the hot chocolate. In what ways did the stick say something about the young people's own experience with loneliness?

They went around the group, each person sharing a time of loneliness. The worship leader then asked the teenagers to make a mosaic on the floor in the middle of the circle with their sticks. What way could they relate the sticks to God's answer for loneliness? This group formed a cross.

The youth concluded this part of their worship with a prayer circle in which each person asked God for his presence in moments of loneliness.

MAKING DECISIONS

There was a certain tension in the group. It was still fall; the seniors in the youth fellowship were uncomfortable. They were faced with many decisions for their futures. One or two were confused by the fact that they would soon be registering for the draft, but most of them were concerned about college choices. Several would be making vocational leaps shortly and two or three were even considering marriage. It seemed fitting to make this type of decision an important realm of their prayer focus.

After the group had sung several popular Christian songs, the youth adviser told the story of Jesus in the garden before his arrest (Matthew 26:36-46 and Luke 22:39-46). Martha, the group leader, lifted up the struggle Jesus faced with his decision to follow the path before him. Beads of sweat fell from his body like blood as Jesus wrestled with this decision.

Martha asked each person to find a separate space on the floor. Then she passed out five colored attachable beads to each person. These beads symbolized Jesus' sweat at his time of decision. Martha asked each person to assume the position of prayer and to assign to each bead a decision which must be made by him or her in the next 12 months. If there were fewer than five difficult decisions, they were encouraged to focus on only the number of beads needed.

Soft music was played in the background as the teenagers moved the beads around and focused on their own decisions. Martha had everyone go around the group and share the decisions represented by the beads.

Martha read the passage she had related to earlier. The worshipers were asked to arrange the beads in order of difficulty with the most perplexing first. These were shared throughout the group.

The group concluded by praying in a circle about each person's most difficult decision. The persons were then asked to carry that bead in their pocket or purse during the next week. Martha was pleased by how focused the prayers were once they had shared the problems with the group. The process seemed to give the prayer a much deeper perspective.

IDENTITY

The Sunday morning class had been dealing with the question, "Who am I?" The youth adviser was amazed over the discussion this topic raised. It seemed that just about everyone was struggling with self-identity and esteem.

It was decided that this concern should be dealt with through worship. The Gospel helps us focus this quest with an additional question: "Whose am I?" The worship leader, Hugh, found a very simple puzzle among the Sunday school materials; it featured a picture of Jesus. This resource was apparently designed for children's use. The pieces were larger than those of most adult puzzles. (You can make your own puzzle from a poster of Jesus.)

The worship leader moved in front of each person and asked him or her to choose a piece from the unassembled puzzle. Hugh had the youth look carefully at the piece and reflect on how this piece was like them in some way.

The final act of prayer was to put the pieces together in the center of the circle. This was worked into the bigger picture.

When the youth had finished and the face of Jesus appeared, they went around the circle, offering prayers for their own quests to find the person God had created through Jesus Christ.

FAMILY RELATIONSHIPS

At the end of a study on family relationships, the worship service focused on the attitudes of the youth concerning their parents. The youth couldn't control their parents, but God can help the youth control their own feelings.

The worship leader, Jane, read the commandment, "Honor your father and your mother" (Exodus 20:12). Jane passed around an apple and asked the worshipers to share ways by which this piece of fruit symbolized a family.

One person said that it looked good on the outside, but it might be rotten on the inside. He indicated that families are the same way. They may give the appearance that everything is fine on the outside and be terrible on the inside.

Another worshiper said that seeds fall out of an apple when it is cut into two pieces. She suggested that the same thing happens when there is a divorce—the children are the seeds which are lost.

Jane reread Exodus 20:12, noting that teenagers can't change parents, but God can change how teenagers present themselves in their families. She passed the apple around again and invited each person to report how the piece of fruit, in some way, represents how God's help can change his or her actions during family problems.

A meaningful period of sharing followed in which the study came into focus. When the final period of prayer came, each person asked God to change him or her in relationship to his or her family.

STRONGER FAITH

A speaker for the evening group led a discussion on the nature of faith. The youth admitted that it was sometimes difficult to remain stable. Dry spells in believing came to even the most faithful person. Everyone agreed that there were times of testing in his or her faith.

At the worship service, the teenage leader passed around a pencil and paper. He read John 20:29, telling the group that the quest for faithfulness covers every moment. Even the most depressing periods in our lives are times when Christ is present.

The prayer of petition was expressed by their composition of a cinquain poem. This form of poetry is an easy way for people to share their complex feelings and is particularly helpful in preparing prayers. The cinquain is created by following these five steps:

1. Title (noun or one word).
2. Two words that describe the title.
3. Three words that are action words or a phrase about the title.
4. Four words that depict a feeling about the title.
5. One word that summarizes the title.

The passage was reread and each person read his or her cinquain. One junior high member wrote the following prayer of petition about her faith:

Faith

yesterday, tomorrow

constantly flicking brightly

sad, longing, hopeful, constant

Jesus

The poems were shared within the group. The youth offered positive responses to the poems of others. The worship leader read the passage again and each person offered his or her prayer of petition by reading the cinquain a second time.

OVERCOMING REJECTION

The youth group members in a church in Delaware were upset by a visitor who said their group was a very unfriendly one. The visitor had only once attended the group; however, he sent back the message that he felt rejected by them.

The talk about this failure surprised the fellowship since they thought things were going so well. When the discussion became more personal, everyone in the youth group admitted that the reality of rejection was his or her greatest fear.

The youth adviser picked up on this theme for the evening worship service. During the prayer act of petition, the group focused on personal rejection.

The leader asked the students to form a tight circle by wrapping their arms around their neighbors—the typical way they ended their meetings. He chose one person to be excluded from the circle. The leader had the worshipers sing the phrase, "Hear our prayer, o Lord," over and over again.

This "excluded" person was encouraged to break into the circle while the others tried to keep him out. After a couple minutes of failure, the worshipers were asked to break the human ring and sit in a circle on the floor.

The excluded member of their group was then asked how it felt to be kept out of the fellowship. Each person in the circle then shared a time in his or her life when he or she experienced exclusion.

The group members concluded with a prayer circle focusing on the needs of each person experiencing rejection. They also pledged to reach out to the rejected young man at school in the upcoming week.

FACING FAILURE

Allan, the president of a Wisconsin youth group, opened the prayer act of petition by holding a large bowl over his head. He mentioned that it had been carefully formed and glazed by a local artist.

Allan then brought the bowl down vigorously and broke it on the floor. He made sure that it broke in a wastepaper basket with a brick in the bottom so that none of the pieces flew on the worshipers.

Allan passed the basket around the circle and asked each person to pick out a piece of the broken bowl. He asked the youth to look at the piece of broken china and compare the piece to a specific time when they felt failure.

These stories were then shared. It was clear that a lot of pain and fear from these moments still existed within these young people. The pieces were placed on the table. Using glue, the youth tried to reassemble the bowl. They talked about how things changed when fear takes over. The bowl, for example, could never be the same. A new bowl, like a new dream, had to replace what was broken. Their closing circle prayer focused on asking God to take control of their fears.

FINDING LOVE

The New York youth group always talked about dating and other matters concerning love during their meetings. It was obvious that love was a major need for these young people.

The youth officers decided to confront this issue in the worship service. When they performed the prayer act of petition, they passed around a small, heart-shaped pillow. Each person was given an opportunity to share the greatest aspect of love.

The worship leader read 1 Corinthians 13. Each person was offered a small candy heart and allowed an opportunity to express one quality of Christian love he or she found attractive.

CONFRONTING DISAPPOINTMENT

Disappointment or guilt is an easy feeling to experience during adolescence. Young people often feel bad about things beyond their control. Their own aspirations or expectations for themselves are almost impossible to fulfill.

One group focused on the prayer act of petition by inviting each person to look at the palm of his or her hand. One member quietly played a familiar hymn on his guitar. The group members were encouraged to look at their palms as if they were a map of their accomplishments. The worship leader was careful not to read palms, an art often associated with cults. She simply invited the worshipers to study their palm lines as a way to reflect on the course of their lives.

After two or three minutes, the youth formed pairs and shared their thoughts about what the lines suggested in terms of tasks not accomplished. How did they feel about falling short of their expectations?

These reflections were shared with the entire group. The worship leader went to each person and asked him or her to offer a prayer for himself or herself. She then rubbed hand lotion on both hands of the youth and assured each one that God would hear his or her prayer.

SEEKING PERSONAL POTENTIAL

The youth group led the youth Sunday service in their Chicago church. They did not change the traditional order of the service; however, when they reached the prayer of petition, they did something which many have never forgotten.

Several members of the group distributed corn kernels to each person in the pews by using collection plates. The worship leader, Ken, asked the congregation to focus on the small amount of corn in their hands. He asked them to pretend that the kernel represented a parable. In what ways does it symbolize our own potential?

Ken read the parable of the mustard seed. While the group was being led in this imaginative prayer act, a corn popper was working at one side of the worship center.

The freshly popped corn was piled on the collection plates and distributed to the worshipers! Ken asked them to seek God for the protection and release of their individual potential. As a symbol of their search, Ken encouraged them to eat their popped corn.

GLORY OF GOD

The South Carolina youth group was spending a retreat weekend in a beautiful mountain setting. One morning they were worshiping outside on a high hill. The air was cool and the sky was sunny with large, billowing clouds.

The worship leader read Psalm 8:1. Then he asked the youth to stretch out on their backs and look into the sky; the clouds were particularly active and colorful.

The leader went around the group asking each person to point out a cloud formation which suggested a teaching about the glory of God. Then each person was asked to offer a prayer of petition requesting the reality of God's glory to come into his or her life.

The experience was so amazing, it left the group members speechless as they headed for breakfast.

PETITION FOR JOY

Dave was a member of an Austin youth group and a fan of science fiction. He particularly liked the novel **Stranger in a Strange Land.** It is the story of Mike and the Martian world. In this world, water is greatly treasured. To share this precious commodity, the inhabitants form a "water kinship." In such a relationship, the participants are able to understand each other fully or grok. There is joy in the fact that one has become united with another.

One week, Dave had the responsibility for the Sunday evening worship service. He decided to utilize this concept so the group could better deal with the imagery of John 4:7-15.

Dave had the young people form a circle. The group sat on the floor in the dimly lighted storage room. When the participants came to the prayer act of petition, Dave passed a bowl of water around and asked each person to hold it while sharing about a time when water brought him or her great joy or comfort.

Dave read John 4:7-15 and told the story of Mike and the bonding of mutual joy in the water ceremony. Dave then asked each person to offer a prayer of petition concerning his or her personal joy before drinking from the bowl. Dave knew the group members might be worried about germs if they shared a common drinking bowl, so he used small communion cups.

FACING THE FUTURE

The group was on a Sunday afternoon hike, walking along the shore of a large lake. This would be the last meeting before some of the members returned to college. The adult leader, Ron, knew the 15 young people very well and he led them in a simple service which utilized the setting.

Ron gathered several handfuls of flat stones. He formed the worshipers in a semicircle facing the water; they sang several songs. Ron then told the people that it was time to pray for their futures. This prayer would be conducted by having each person throw a flat stone into the water. Ron showed these people how to make the stones skip across the surface. The person throwing the stone would then share how the action of the stone symbolized something about his or her future.

This was an extremely moving event. After everyone had shared, the members held hands and conducted a prayer circle focusing on each person's needs to face the unknown future.

SPIRITUAL ZEAL

Several members of a youth group in Arizona admitted that they overexerted as far as involvement in church activities was concerned. These were the youth who seemed to spend all their time at the church. School activities were now interfering with church activities and these young people were thinking of dropping out of their group. Other people had similar comments. How could they keep their spiritual zeal?

The group members focused on prayer for an answer. When they came to the prayer acts of petition, each person was invited to walk to the center of the circle. The youth was handed a club made by rolled newspapers and masking tape. Also in the center was a sawhorse. The leader

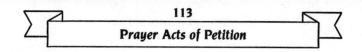

asked the person to say the Lord's Prayer aloud; however, the teenager had to hit the sawhorse with as much power as possible.

It was amazing how the energy increased with this emphatic repeating of the Lord's Prayer. The students then formed a circle of prayer, focusing on their personal needs in their quest of faithfulness.

CHAPTER 9

Prayer Acts of Thanksgiving

Nothing warms the human heart more than the giving and receiving of Christian love. The act of thanking someone satisfies both the bearer of appreciation and the receiver of it. Of course, our prayer relationship with God is different than thanking a favorite aunt for the special treat she gave us.

There is something extremely satisfying for the worshiper to express his or her thanks to God. Perhaps the very act of giving thanks is a way of asserting our faith. Thanksgiving can truly be an act of making a faith statement.

When I thank God for another day or for the love of my family, I am confessing my dependence on God and submitting my life to him. It is wondrous to fall before God and feel the love and care of my creator. I always feel a sense of awe and wonder that such a being could listen to me.

Prayer acts of thanksgiving are the most refreshing aspects of faith. I am always amazed that there is more for which to be thankful than I had imagined. Perhaps God speaks to us in this prayer act for this reason.

Moments of greatest difficulty, pain and tears have often been moments of intense prayers of thanksgiving. Why are we most touched when we acknowledge the goodness of God?

The purpose of this part of the service is to give the worshiper an opportunity to thank God for his gifts. How do we experience this exchange between the giver of life and the receiver? Following are 15 examples of creative thanksgiving prayer acts.

THE SIMPLEST GIFTS OF NATURE

The regional camp program was exceptional. The director had researched the history of the region and had been able to resurrect the customs of the native people. The director found that part of the camping area had been built along the lines of the original Indian dwellings.

During the thanksgiving prayer act at one of their services, the director told of how the original inhabitants of this area felt a special bond with nature. It was their conviction that God created even the smallest creatures. They acknowledged even the grass and other aspects of nature.

These early Indians wore a special leather strip on their moccasins. The strip was a prayer of thanksgiving for the blades of grass and small insects which were accidently destroyed as the Indians walked upon the earth.

The director went to the members of the group and put leather strips around their shoes. He asked them to walk around the area for a couple minutes in silence.

The group members then reconvened and shared their prayers of thanks for all things which must be sacrificed in order for the students to live. The group members took the leather strips with them as a reminder that life is a gift from God.

THE SAINTS WHO HAVE DIED

An Iowa youth group developed a very special thanksgiving worship tradition to remember those from the congregation who had died.

Members of the family were personally invited to this service. They were asked what kind of tree they would prefer to have for this thanksgiving prayer service. The tree was then purchased and a large hole dug.

The youth held the service at the planting site. The young people leading the service asked those attending for

stories and thanks for the deceased person's life. As the
tree was planted, the members of the youth group shared a
short prayer for the witness of the deceased sister or
brother.

*"Lord God, we saw our faithful parents fall by the tree of
temptation in the garden of Eden. We have also experienced the forgiveness and resurrection confirmed by
Christ." "We plant this tree as an act of thanksgiving for
this special life of our brother/sister_____.
May this tree proudly bear witness to your faithfulness to
him/her. This we ask in the name of Jesus Christ.
Amen."*

These living memorials of thanksgiving played a very
meaningful role in the life of the congregation. This worship model is important because it once again shows how
youth can minister to the entire church through worship.

THE PASTOR

When the fellowship group conducted the Sunday
morning youth service with the youth adviser in charge,
the pastor took the Sunday off. The youth really appreciated how the pastor had worked on their behalf.

The youth had developed a very meaningful prayer act
of thanksgiving for the pastor's ministry. During the prayer
of thanksgiving, the youth passed out cards. The teenagers
took turns bearing testimony of thanksgiving concerning
the pastor. The youth then asked the people to write a note
of thanksgiving for the ministry of the pastor. These notes
were collected.

The group left the thank-you notes on the pastor's
desk. It was a surprising and special moment for the pastor
when he found them.

GOD'S ABIDING LOVE

Frank, the youth adviser for the Missouri church, collected fossils as a hobby. The worship team focused on this
hobby and Psalm 79:13 for a service. The writer affirmed
that the people would thank God forever "... from generation to generation we will recount thy praise."

When the group came to the thanksgiving prayer act in the Sunday evening service, Frank passed a fossil around and read Psalm 79:13.

Each person was asked what God was telling him or her about the thanksgiving perspective through this fossil. One teenager said that the pieces of preserved life show that we need to be thankful for everyone's contribution to our faith. Another member of the group suggested that God is extremely patient with us.

Frank passed the fossil around again and asked each person to identify something in the fossil which exemplified the gift of someone in the group. One person said that the shell reminded him of Ann's perseverance in planning the programs. Another girl shared that the partial exposure of one ancient animal is like a mystery which members of the group have yet to reveal to each other.

They closed in a circle thanking God for his endless love from generation to generation.

THE BREATH OF LIFE

It was a cool fall day. The youth group had joined with two others and took a trip to a nearby hospital. After visiting with the residents, the group gathered for refreshments, debriefing and worship. The experience had been very deep; the older people were fun to work with, as they enjoyed talking with the youth. But the group was struck by the way these older people were suffering physically.

The host church was in charge of the worship service. The teenagers leading the service encouraged the other youth to gather outside behind the church. It was slightly chilly, but not uncomfortable. When the youth came to the prayer acts of thanksgiving, Jane, the leader, told them that God's greatest gift was the breath of life (Genesis 2:7). The Holy Spirit is often perceived as breath or wind in the New Testament. We are alive physically and spiritually through the breath of God; yet, we are just one breath of air away from death.

Jane asked the worshipers to hold their breath until she indicated to them to let go. Jane did this herself so that she could more easily tell how to instruct the others. When she told them to breathe, each person was glad to take a fresh breath.

Jane went around the group and encouraged each person to share a time when he or she thought he or she would become breathless. What was that first full breath like? Several students had experienced nearly fatal water accidents; many youth had had the "wind knocked out of them."

Then a prayer circle was formed in which every person was invited to thank God for the breath of life. Jane asked each person to conclude his or her prayer by expelling a long breath into the air. The cold late afternoon made it possible to see each person's breath; this became a visual amen.

SPIRITUAL KINSHIP

In a study of Genesis 2 and other key passages, the youth group discovered the important Old Testament concept of *nephesh*. This word is often translated as "soul." However, it has a very important meaning in its biblical context. The term denotes the state of being totally human by being a member of the spiritual community.

For example, when a person was welcomed into the tent of another, the guest became part of the spiritual kinship with the host. If the guest was killed, the host would have the same responsibilities of revenge as if the victim had been a blood relative. This scholarly approach soon became practical once the worship team began working on the service.

During the thanksgiving prayer acts, the worship team decided to focus on the spiritual kinship God had given the group. As the youth were gathered in a circle, they held hands. The leader, Joe, reemphasized the gift of being a living spiritual community. He asked each worshiper to give thanks for a specific gift which the person next to him or her contributed to the kinship.

This portion of the service was closed by singing a hymn focusing on the role of the breath of God in the spiritual community. Joe went behind the circle and gently blew the *nephesh* on the back of each person's head.

INDIVIDUAL DIFFERENCES

The Pennsylvania church is in a college town and takes its ministry with college youth very seriously. The minister and his wife host a special annual celebration the second Friday in October which lifts up thanks for the special gifts of the students. ''The Night of the Great Pumpkin'' was inspired by the popular comic strip ''Peanuts.''

These people have found that nearby farmers are happy to get rid of the misshapen, unripened little pumpkins. The youth began the evening by passing out panels from the Peanuts comic strip. Each person was asked to share the ways by which the strip reflected something we should be thankful for.

The pumpkins were placed in the middle of the room and each person was asked to choose one. The pastor asked the students to spend a few minutes familiarizing them-selves with their pumpkins and reflecting on how the pumpkins, in some way, symbolized something about the students.

The students then showed their vegetables to the group and related their insights on how their personal individ-uality and the uniqueness of their pumpkins coincided. There is always a surprising discussion as people talk about how personal differences are often criticized in social circles.

The evening was closed with a prayer thanking God for the gift of uniqueness. The hosts then invited the students to take the pumpkins with them.

THE GIFT OF PLAY

During the evening worship service, the president of the youth group celebrated the prayer of thanksgiving by passing out several toy catalogs. He asked each person to find a picture of a toy and tear it out of the publication.

The members shared the emotions the toy had created for them when they were younger. Then the members talked about the role of play in their present lives. Why is such a childlike gift from God important to the older teenagers and adults?

The group closed in a circle of prayer focusing on thanking God for the gift of play.

SIMPLE THINGS

The high school class had been studying the creation stories in Genesis. For the prayer, Sally decided to focus on thankfulness for God's creation. She gave each person a piece of modeling clay and read Genesis 1:9-13.

She asked the group members to each make a shape symbolizing something in their lives for which they were most thankful. After expressing their thankfulness through their creations, she invited the students to arrange the clay sculptures on the table in the center of the circle.

They closed by praying in a circle, focusing on thankfulness for these aspects of God's creation.

PERSONAL THINGS

One Portland youth group has an interesting tradition. They assign members certain parts of the weekly fellowship worship service. For example, a youth group member named Mike had the prayer acts of thanksgiving for six weeks.

Mike started an interesting way of drawing people into this type of prayer. He brought one of his mother's finest silver bowls and passed it around the prayer circle. Each person was given the opportunity to name something which might be put in the bowl as the symbol of his or her prayer of thanksgiving to God.

Mike then gave the bowl to a person named Ann and told her to return it the following week with something for which she was thankful. This person returned the following week with a single flower bud floating in water. She told the group about the beauty of the rose. It was an important symbol to her because she used to assist her late father in caring for roses.

Mike passed the bowl around. People prayed for Ann

and thanked her for sharing such beautiful memories.

Mike passed the bowl on to someone else to take care of the thanksgiving prayer act for the following week.

THE COUNTRY

One evening, a youth group in Pittsburgh left their meeting area in the church basement and went to the cemetery next door. It was close to Memorial Day. The graveyard had many plots of fallen soldiers, with graves tracing back to the American Revolution.

Tony, a worship leader who gathered with the youth in the military burial area, carried the American flag from the sanctuary. Tony told the rest of the students to focus their prayer of thanksgiving on a particular person who was buried near them. Each person was to find one person's headstone. After a few minutes, the youth would reconvene and be asked to share the life of the person they chose.

When they reconvened, Tony gave each person a chance to take the group to his or her choice of tombstone. Using the data from the tombstone, the young person would introduce the deceased and express some reasons why he or she was thankful for his or her life.

The participants expressed thanksgiving for those who had given their lives. However, they also struggled with the question of why many young people die in wars. Almost every stone indicated that young people had been killed in these different wars.

To close the worship, each person held on to an edge of the flag and offered prayers of thanksgiving.

THE SUFFERING OF OTHERS

Dan, a pop star, told me that he was overwhelmed by his visit to the small Vincent van Gogh museum. "As I went through those rooms of pictures, I kept thinking, 'Thank you, man—thank you.' I could see so much suffering in this man's spirit. Since he had endured this suffering and expressed himself so I could experience his feelings, it meant that I would not have to go through it."

The suffering of Jesus is a gift for Christians. Dan's comment and the promise of John 3:16 were ringing in my head when I put together the youth group's worship service. I passed around my copy of Vincent van Gogh's "Starry Night."

The group was given a chance to share the kinds of emotions they could discern from the painting. How did the suffering and confusing expressed in this painting help the group to experience the same suffering?

I passed around a small wooden statue of Jesus which someone from Poland had given me. I read the story of how God gave his only son so that we might have eternal life (John 3:16). The group members were asked to share the ways through which Christ specifically provided for them.

We closed with a prayer circle in which everyone thanked God for the ministry and witness of others.

JESUS

A Dearborn youth group had invited another church to share the programs for the six-week period prior to Easter. They were studying the nature of Christ.

For the worship experience one evening, the planning team had collected every possible picture of Jesus; they raided the Sunday school storage closets at both churches.

The team was able to give each person a picture of Jesus. For the prayer act of thanksgiving, the worship leader distributed the pictures and asked the youth to focus on them. The leader asked the participants what was one attribute about Jesus which was triggered by looking at him.

Each person shared his or her picture and related the things about Jesus for which he or she was most thankful. After each contribution, the rest of the worshipers repeated, "Hear our thanksgiving, o Lord."

FOOD

The act of eating together is significant. Most youth groups just skip from program to refreshments without giving this part of the gathering much thought. A youth fellowship in Spokane takes this part of their life together seriously. Every time they eat as a group, they also include a worship act. They call these thanksgiving prayer acts "table devotions."

For example, after a program which focused on the "fruits of the Spirit," the group members passed out pieces of fruit. They went around the circle and asked each person to share the ways through which his or her piece of fruit symbolized something for which he or she needed to be thankful to God.

The worship leader then collected the pieces of fruit and cut them into slices; a huge fruit salad was created. Before they ate this delicious and healthy treat, they formed a prayer circle focusing on thanksgiving for God's gifts of the Spirit.

THE BIRTH OF JESUS

At the last meeting before Christmas, a New York youth group added a special element to their worship. During the prayer of thanksgiving, they gathered in a tight circle.

The teenage worship leader read the account of Mary learning about the forthcoming birth of her child (Luke 1:26-38). He then passed around a baby blanket with lightly sprinkled baby powder.

The youth were asked to smell the baby blanket and share their thoughts about how Mary must have felt upon hearing the message of Gabriel. What did she fear?

The leader passed the blanket around again and asked the group to think about the kind of thanksgiving prayer Mary would have shared. The group closed the service with words of thanksgiving for the gift of the Christ child.

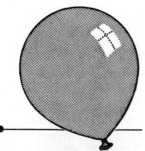

CHAPTER 10

Music in Worship

At the very moment of creation there was music as the wind moved across the face of the waters. The beat of the heart is musical. Some even say that the source of music is the heartbeat. Every living creature participates in the music of nature.

Human history reveals both the creative use and disappointing abuse of music. The children of Israel could sing and use tambourines, harps, flutes and lyres in worship of the Lord God. However, their pagan neighbors also utilized these gifts to accompany human sacrifice and other abuses of worship.

The early church enjoyed music in worship with the singing of hymns and psalms. The history of the church is rich with the variety and creativity of writers and performers. The church has often been the patron of the musical art form at key points in history. For example, the church of the Middle Ages (classical) and the American church (Gospel) have played a major role in the preservation of music.

CHURCH AND WORLD

There has always been a fluid relationship between sacred and secular music. At points of artistic interest and evangelical outreach, the Christian community has been eager to embrace secular music forms to reach out to unbelievers. In the classical period, secular writers provided the church with the best compositions. Struggling

composers needed the commissions from these compositions to survive. Great musicians and singers were utilized
in the worship of God.

During the eras of intense evangelism, popular secular
tunes were transformed into religious songs in order to
confront people in the world with the message of Christ.
These evangelists didn't care if the music had been previously known as a saloon ballad. As long as the new
words focused on Christ, it would be used.

There have been tensions over the use of music
throughout the history of the Christian church. There are
still faith traditions which do not permit instrumental
music in Christian worship. If you are involved in those
traditions, I hope that you will stay with us for the discussion and ideas in this chapter. There will be ideas which
can be used in your settings.

Psalms seem to have been accepted for worship by
most people. In fact, some of the hymnals from the frontier
church contained split pages. The metered words of the
Psalms were on one half of the page while the tunes were
on the other half. This enabled the worshipers to exchange
words and tunes.

IN OUR DAY

Youth ministry still runs into trouble with "youth worship." Often adults express discomfort over changes in
traditional worship by focusing on "modern" music. Many
young people have come to me in tears over this matter.
"My brother-in-law warns me that I am giving in to the
devil because I'm listening to contemporary Christian
music."

Fortunately, many churches are using modern Christian
music regularly in their services. People can no longer
blame the youth for changes. As I have discussed in an
earlier chapter, *adults* are now demanding changes.
Whatever the case, change in worship is a most sensitive
matter.

Many choir directors simply do not work well with
youth. There are some who only value those with natural
musical talent. This elitist attitude can be damaging to
youth in traditional worship. However, there are people

like Walter Horsley, who claims that he started out trying to get youth and others to sing beautiful music. He has learned that his real ministry is to help youth become more beautiful as persons of faith.

If you are a youth adviser in a church without a serious youth music program, you will need to move carefully to bring your expertise into practice. You have so much to offer the other staff in the church. The special relationship you have with the young people is an incredible gift of God. I pray that you are in a working context where you can exercise this gift in every part of the church's life as it touches the lives of the young. You are the most important advocate for lively worship in the congregation.

SING A NEW SONG

Singing is rooted deep in human history. Indeed, some think that speech was first a chanting or songlike pattern. Worship in the Old and New Testament is constantly related to singing; it is a primary way to praise God.

Early liturgies featured chanting and singing. People who could not read could learn the liturgy if it was sung.

The evangelistic explosions in the history of the faith have found that singing in worship is most effective. Unions also discovered the unifying power of music. After studying the ebb and flow of union strength, a sociologist concluded that group singing was common during periods of real union strength. In fact, they used popular church hymns with altered lyrics. On the other hand, the sociologist found that when workers stopped singing together at meetings, the union movement was at its weakest.

These notes raise two points. On the one hand, these youth have something important to bring to the faith community: strong and vital congregational singing. Youth may provide the spark to this aspect of traditional worship. On the other hand, the increase in hired choirs and reduced participation by worshipers may suggest that group singing is no longer a valid form of corporate worship. We may have moved into a spectator generation of adults; mass media does it all for us. This may be too radical a conclusion; yet, the role of music in worship is at a critical stage.

The problem is more than the addition of new songs, more instruments or bigger choirs will resolve.

There are some especially bright spots on the liturgical tapestry of worship and music. Avery and Marsh, and Yohann Anderson are three examples of a special breed of Christian enablers who have helped to lead us out of the liturgical crisis facing many congregations.

Richard Avery and Donald Marsh are an incredible local church pastor and music director team who have combined the very best in authentic and creative worship. They use humor, the senses and every resource God has given us to worship. They write original music which is simple and theologically sound. I particularly appreciate their ability to take historical forms and help us relate to them with freshness and joy.

Yohann Anderson is a special combination of many different gifts. He is a talented youth worker and teacher. The biggest contribution he has made to the contemporary church is that he has taken the mystery out of singing in worship. In his opinion, God has created everyone for the purpose of singing a new song. It is amazing to see the walls of hesitation fall away as he works with a group. If you can hum, Yohann will enable you to worship God with your voice. As a non-singer, I find that he has encouraged me to sing a joyous song even if I can't sing in key. His book, **Songs**, is a lasting resource for youth ministry.

CHOOSING MUSIC FOR WORSHIP

There is no problem finding contemporary music. Just about everyone seems to be writing youth music, and you are probably using this kind of material currently. But I do think that a youth group should be selective about this material. Since I am not a musician, I will not judge the musical quality of contemporary worship music. However, I find many of the lyrics offensive. Too many of these songs feature egocentric theology. In my opinion, there are three common flows in much of contemporary Christian music:

1. Simplicity. The lyrics tend to lean in the direction of TV jingles; perhaps they are written this way intentionally. Who can forget these addictive tunes after 50 exposures? I know that many chantings are simple series of phrases.

Yet, many youth groups may find themselves being spiritually raised with worship songs which have almost no theological content. I do not believe that worship songs need to be "developed" creeds. Yet, we come to worship God who acts in history and meets us in the complexity of life.

2. Jesus-ology. I remember Martin Marty's comment after a well-known Christian musician finished singing his popular contemporary songs. "From what I just heard, the score is Jesus—5, church—0." Marty noted the emphasis on "Jesus and me." There seems to be an understanding of and respect for the Trinity. We need to celebrate Christ's birth (Father), ministry, death and Resurrection (Jesus), and the formation of the Christian community (Holy Spirit) in order to be authentic biblically.

3. Individualistic. One of the biggest criticisms of contemporary Christian music is its tendency to be extremely individualistic. Again, this may go back to the pietistic tradition, which linked the believer's personal relationship to Jesus. Yet, for Christian youth, it is important that they proclaim their faith in relationship to the faith family. By this, I mean that we worship as part of a 4,000-year history. I am a person, unique and special. I am linked to the kinship of God through the work of the Holy Spirit; I am known by God through my membership in this community.

I hope that you don't think I am being critical of all contemporary worship music. I merely suggest caution in making your decisions about contemporary music. Some may think that getting a group to sing in worship is a value in itself. In the end, it will be God who judges the purity of our hearts and the integrity of our worship.

I will explore 10 areas of consideration which should be probed in the use of music in creative worship. These are some things taking place around the world as Christians gather to Worship God.

WRITING OUR OWN WORSHIP SONGS

If you are non-musical (like me), you may think that such an idea is beyond the reach of your youth ministry. However, I bet that there is someone in your group or in your community who can help your youth create their own musical confession of faith. I have found that God always provides someone with the abilities I lack. Perhaps God has called those of us without certain skills in order to permit others to do their ministry. This means that you are not called because of musical ability. God has you working with youth for a purpose according to your gifts.

You may have seen how easy it is to sing the doxology to the music of pop tunes. The same process is possible with words which you write. It will take a bit of juggling, but you can use anything from a pop tune to an old hymn for your music base. For example, one group of first-grade teachers in New York took the song, "If You're Happy and You Know It," and created these worship lyrics:

"If you're sorry and you know it, nod your head

If you're sorry and you know it, not your head

If you're sorry and you know it, you really need to show it.

If you're sorry and you know it, nod your head."

Their Ash Wednesday service opened with these lines and then closed with the following lyrics and same tune:

"Now that you love God, clap your hands

Now that you love God, clap your hands

Now that you love God, you can go in peace

Now that you love God, clap your hands."

Many youth conferences commission a musician who will be performing at the event to write a song for the occasion. The song is used over and over to tie the singing experience into the content of the gathering.

Some youth groups like to use the basic music of their tradition; however, you should consider changing some of the sexist language. When men and women are singing together before God, there is simply no excuse to utilize sexual references which are unfounded.

Don't overlook the musical talent of your teenagers. In one Pennsylvania group, a teenager wrote a special closing "amen" musical piece which was used every week.

MUSICAL MOTION

A Pittsburgh church has had a "motion" choir for some years. This choir involves people doing arm motions to the lyrics of the hymn; it is not a dance. The impressive aspect of this particular worship model is that their choir has a Down's-syndrome child as a member. This handicapped teenager can participate in the worship of God through this approach.

Find a dance coach or theater director in the community or church to help your group work on "hymns in motion." Once you have developed the music in motion, ask for inclusion of this youth contribution at one of the church seasons. The congregation is always willing for something special during Advent and Lent.

There are also a number of "action" songs which youth worship settings tend to utilize. This use of music encourages the youth to follow the motions of the leader in the course of singing. The intention is to get teenagers to interact and become a community. Avery and Marsh have introduced motion groups for years and find almost no negative reaction. They simply use the basic hymns and teach the congregation four or five arm positions which are indicated by certain phrases. For example, "Holy Spirit" might be represented by holding the palms in front of you. This works very well with familiar hymns. Adding motion to the music also brings a rush of interest and vitality to the worshipers. It is striking how much meaning is experienced by moving to the words.

MUSIC WITH SIGNING

A number of secular groups have formed "signing" choirs. These choirs are composed of those who use the signing language developed by deaf people. They play popular songs and all of them sign out the lyrics. This is a particularly touching way to experience music.

I trust that there are several young people in your youth group who already know how to do sign language. Take the traditional hymns and teach the teenagers to sing and do the signs by having one of the youth lead the group in worship. He can stop singing one verse and continue to sign it. Imagine an evening in which you invite someone from the community (perhaps a deaf person) to present the program and then lead the worship service.

This model can be used both as a technique for presenting worship music, or the group can develop signing to be used with the congregation or elsewhere. Whenever we can enable and equip youth for ministry, we should utilize that opportunity to strengthen the ministry of youth. This model also works well with the reading of Bible verses and repeating prayers and creeds.

LINING MUSIC

During the frontier days, many churches did not have hymnals, so the song leader simply spoke the line before it was sung. This sounds like a difficult timing problem; however, it works extremely well.

I believe that there is a great advantage in using music in this way. Something seems to be missing when I look at a group singing with their heads buried in books or song sheets. Why not try the lining method? Then the singers can clap, hold hands or actually look at the other believers.

Some youth workers use overhead projectors and other projection forms to show the lyrics before the worshiping youth. One must be careful to check whether everyone can see the screen and read the words. I have been in large settings where the singing dies because no one can read the screen.

DANCE

There are some churches which do not permit their people to dance. We know that there is a long history of dance as part of worship. The ancient Jews danced to praise the Lord; yet, there have always been pagan or secular forms of dance which made the people of faith uncomfortable. Dance can praise or ridicule the Lord. The tradition that danced to praise God also used dance as a way to kill John the Baptist.

There are many exciting ways for music and dance to combine for authentic and powerful worship experiences. For instance, I was a speaker at a Jewish temple. After I finished, I was very impressed to see how the young people immediately began to do biblical dances. They provided their own music because they often sang while they danced. I was pleased that vigorous dances were used. I object to dancing in churches when it is individual or limited to couples.

It would be interesting to invite a nearby Jewish youth group or leader to come and teach your people these fine dances. One could then incorporate the dances in the weekly worship service.

Many teenagers in youth groups are finely trained dancers. It is quite moving to see someone dance Psalm 23 in worship. Use these models in your own youth services if the Sunday morning experience is not open to this form.

I have seen groups do a call to worship by using a secular dance like the bunny hop! There is something important about using a physically demanding activity such as the bunny hop for the prelude or introduction to worship. Again, you could add words to the basic bunny hop. This would mean that your youth would be gathering for worship by using both their mouths and entire bodies.

Some people in Illinois worship by using an extremely small amount of movement. The pastor asked the people to stand with their feet shoulders-width apart. They swayed slightly as they read the scripture antiphonally and moved to the rhythm of the reading. This chanting style of reading and moving creates an amazing sense of unity.

SPECIAL SINGING

I am continually delighted by what talented people can do with almost any kind of worship music. You have probably used music by which the worshipers can sing rounds or overlapping verses. There are numerous ways this type of group singing can be varied. It is important that you tap someone who has these skills. You can give two or three of your teenagers the opportunity to be trained in leading group singing. Every community has someone with these creative skills.

Some groups utilize humming and other vocal sounds for use in worship. It is amazing how special this becomes for use during prayers and other parts of youth worship. There is almost no limit to the kind of "singing" we can offer the Lord through praise.

Chanting was mentioned earlier. This wonderful way of singing goes back to the earliest days of Christian worship. Millions of Christians still use chanting. You will find ample help from those in your community who have learned this specialized means to worship God.

Youth also have found that by preparing special music presentations, they can actually minister to others. Some have enjoyed performing musicals written especially for youth groups. Most religious music publishers can provide lists of such offerings.

Other youth groups have written their own presentations. One minister writes a musical each year for the youth to present. Dave uses current and traditional songs and weaves them into a short story framework; this presentation has become a highlight of the church year. Through this production, the youth are able to raise money for workcamps and other service projects. While the revue is not technically a worship service, it does focus on Christian themes; and during the closing moments, the whole audience sings with the students.

MUSICAL BACKGROUND

The first youth group I served had a problem because no one could play the piano. We could have just sung without musical background, but this is sometimes difficult when you have a small group. One Atlanta group solved this problem by putting guitar, piano or organ music on audio cassettes.

Many soloists now buy commercial tapes for full musical background. This means that you can nudge youth to sing solo pieces by providing a first-class musical setting; this works extremely well.

Some groups have been even more basic about providing musical backgrounds for their singing. One of the members of a youth fellowship in Texas is a drummer. He did not want to bring the set and play it for worship. However, he found a number of different items which could be used as percussion instruments. He has now organized the youth group so that it can play rhythm on all of its songs; it is remarkably moving.

PLACEMENT OF MUSIC

Music is very portable in worship. There is total flexibility in the placement of the music selections in your order of worship. When can music provide the wings on which the people can be carried closer to God?

There is also the opportunity to move music physically within the worship environment. With a small group, you have many options. Some of the most enriching moments I have experienced in worship have come from singing as we joined hands and moved along as a chain. We have done this along the dunes late at night, through caves and in dark basements. In fact, some youth choirs have performed in worship while standing in the center aisle. They form two lines and face the congregation by standing back to back. This change of location cuts the length of the church in half and puts the music in the midst of the people.

For one youth Sunday, the young people decided to use its strong singers in a very special way. They intentionally placed the members in a scattered pattern throughout the congregation. When it came time to sing the anthem, the youth stood at the pew. This gave the congregation a sense of the group's impact throughout the congregation.

MUSICIANS

There are many talented musicians in every church; however, it is not always easy to get teenagers to play their instrument for Sunday evening worship. One of the reasons for this reluctance is the church's too-common suspicions about musicians. Most churches will accept those who play the piano, organ or trumpet. However, electric guitars, drums and other secular instruments are looked upon with suspicion.

I remember standing with three young people at the end of a worship. "Thank you for this workshop. We play in a combo at the local pizza parlor. The people in church treat us as if we are evil. They are wrong; we love the Lord—why can't we play our music and be Christians?"

One of the best opportunities available for utilizing musicians in youth worship is to invite those from outside the group to share. An Episcopal priest in Alabama met some young people who played in a local restaurant. He asked them if they would write some original music for the Gospel lesson on Christmas Eve. The musicians worked together for several weeks. On the night of the service, the three musicians asked if it would be okay to receive communion.

This story illustrates two important factors in utilizing outside musicians. First, you can tap into incredible talent. Most musicians yearn for an audience; beginning or unknown musicians have few places to play. Secondly, once we receive the gifts of others, they are willing to receive what we have to offer. I call this the ministry of anticipation. Someone has to stand with youth as they get better at their art. Young people send me tapes and beg me to hear their music. I am not a critic; however, I am a listening audience.

There is no form of music or musical instrument which does not have a place in the worship of God. A context has to be created so that the instrument will add to the focus on God. Youth need to be encouraged to share their talents in worship events. Please be patient and remember that youth come to the faith community from a very different kind of world. Perfection is held up as an end in itself for the rest of their lives. The records the youth hear are perfect—after much overdubbing and other criticism; only the best are recognized in the school and society. Yet, when gathering around the Word of God, we are judged from very different standards; the standards are more demanding and less restricting. God beckons the whole person in each of us. You can make noise acceptable to the Lord by playing a kazoo.

One of the miracles of Christian worship is that we gather not only to glorify God, but also to give the Lord everything we have. This means that we are called to expand our creative horizons. As a youth adviser, you are given a challenging role of enabling people to bring all of themselves to Christ; there is nothing more revealing than the sharing of a person's musical offering.

OTHER CULTURES

America is a confederation of many cultures. North

America is filled with people who have come from somewhere else. And each wave of newcomers seems to make the previous wave resentful of their latest neighbors. Some people are critical of the newest to enter our land; what a shame! God has given us an amazing new opportunity to draw upon new gifts from these people.

The great gift of the increases among the black, Latin, Native American and Asian segments of our population (by number or by influence) is that we will have new ingredients to enrich our culture. I am told by Catholic friends that more than half of their church will be Latin by the year 2000. This means changes in our approach to liturgy.

The worship music of these cultures can be a wonderful opportunity for your local youth group. I trust there are black, Latin, Native American and Asian Christians in your community. Invite them to your worship experience and ask them to bring their music and prayers. Teaching has a place in worship; these people can contribute much to such an event.

You may wonder why I included the black community among the people who are new to our land. It is true that the black heritage in America goes back as far as the white. Yet, the black community has preserved a very important musical experience for worship. Most white churches simply have not had the opportunity to use this wondrous musical heritage.

The same kind of comment is due for the Native Americans. They were here before anyone else! Yet, these Americans have a very special perspective concerning nature and life which enriches our understanding of Christ. What a special treat to invite these people to contribute to your worship experience.

Christ is clearly the one who calls all people to worship him. The horn sounds and we drop what we are doing, we forget the color of our skin and come together as the kinship of Christ.

Our young people, more than anyone else in the church, need to know this inclusive experience in worship. Please arrange these culturally rich worship experiences for them. Music can be a rich vehicle for the Spirit to unify those from many lands and walks of life.

CHAPTER 11

The Offering

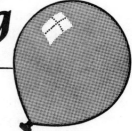

The Christian believes that all things belong to and come from God. We live by the Lord's will; it is through God that we are born, breathe and exist. What can be more proper and fitting than our response to this love by making an offering to him?

Many churches spend a great deal of time urging their people to be more responsive in their giving. The stewardship drive is often the key factor in determining what kind of a programming year the church will have. Some people feel so powerless that they can only show approval or disapproval of leadership through their giving.

On the other hand, some people follow the biblical clue and give 10 percent of everything to God. They do this out of a sense of faithfulness. This dedicated nucleus of people believe that they are blessed by such acts of offering. I remember a woman who attended a small church which I served. When a special mission concern would arise, Jessie would pull me aside, stuff a $20 bill in my hand and ask me to apply the money to the concern. I knew the story of this poor woman's life. She was a licensed practical nurse who supported a disabled husband, her daughter and two grandchildren. When I would try to remind Jessie of her needs, she would always cut me off with an indignant response, "It is a privilege to give to the work of the Lord!"

In many traditions, the offering comes right after the

people have received the Word or Sacrament. This is their response to the many gifts from God.

Many churches are disturbed because adults have found more satisfaction giving their offerings to preachers on television or radio than to home congregations. There are probably many reasons for this trend. The television preacher can control the proposed use of the gifts more vividly than many churches. It seems more satisfying to be moved by a picture of a starving child or building plan than to realize that contributions to the church will help some unknown needy person.

Some critics disregard the people's impulse to give when they see a need on television. "It is just egocentric giving!" This may be the case, but we must accept the fact that it feels good emotionally to place sacrifices before our God.

Does the feeling of completeness, found in the act of giving, always have to be a self-centered act? Doesn't God want us to experience fulfillment through giving? Of course, some of these television people tend to play up the self rewards. "God blessed the man who wrote this letter by returning to him three times what he sent."

Fortunately, many churches do a wonderful job interpreting stewardship. Their people both intellectually and emotionally understand that their contribution to the collection plate is done for the service of God. Yet, most youth do not feel that they have much to give in the adult system. They have little money and do not usually realize that what they have is valued by the local congregation.

The offering time in worship can play an important role in the life of the young Christian. How do we draw youth into responding to God's gift as an act of worship? The offering can be a time when we bring ourselves before God and receive a sense of our worthiness in return. Following are 10 models to help youth experience new meaning for the act of offering.

ANOTHER KIND OF OFFERING ACT WITH MONEY

An Ohio youth group had been studying stewardship. They considered the question, "How do we use what God has given us to serve in his name?" When the time came for the offering on Sunday evening, the young people had a surprise. The offering plate was passed differently. There were envelopes in it; the worship leader asked each person to take one.

When they opened the envelopes, money was inside. Each person seemed to have amounts varying from $1 to $10. The leader asked the congregation to take this symbol of God's gift and invest it in some way so a greater offering could be given during the next service.

There was a great deal of conversation afterward. What could be done with this money? How did God want the congregation to "invest" it? What is an adequate offering for the Lord?

During the next worship, there was much excitement. The teenagers had taken the offering portion of the last service seriously. When offering time came, each person shared what had happened to him or her in the course of investing the offering to God.

Several young people joined together and invested their money and time in a baking project. They proudly placed in the offering plate over $100. This amount had been raised through the sale of baked goods.

Another teenager had printed little notes and put them on the windshields of cars that had overdue time on their parking meters. He put coins from his offering money in the meters for them. The note suggested that if these people appreciated this good deed, they could send a donation to the church. No one responded. He only had a portion of his offering left.

One of the worshipers had given all his offering money to help a program for the hungry.

Then the youth discussed what was a true offering to God. Did God want more or less of one's money or self? The group members planned how they would use the increased amount they had received from the investments of group members, then closed with a prayer for the use of the offering.

THE GIVING OF OUR BODIES

A church in Pennsylvania works closely with the relatives of people waiting for transplant operations. The church has been able to enlist the help of over 100 families willing to give these visitors the hospitality of their homes.

The youth group was involved in this program of caring. At one planning session for worship, they talked about the death of a visitor. The hospital could not find an organ to save the child's life. They were amazed how few adults had signed the permission slip for such a donation upon their death.

From this concern developed an amazing idea for the offering during the youth Sunday service. During the offering, one of the young people told the story of the child who had died without an organ donor. She said that God gave his only begotten Son in order that we might have life. It seems right that we give life to others. The youth then distributed organ donor cards. The worshipers were asked to meditate before the offering was taken. If they felt called upon to give this ultimate gift of life, they were to fill out the cards.

The offering was taken; many people signed the donor cards. This model could be used with the local blood drive as a less dramatic (but equally important) act of offering a gift in response to God's love.

THE OFFERING FROM THE HEART

The youth Sunday service focused on the food outreach to the hungry, sponsored by the church's denomination. In order to build the sensitivity of the congregation during the offering time, the youth used a very basic idea.

During the call to worship, the teenage liturgist informed the congregation that a person dies every eight seconds from starvation. After the announcement, the beat of a bass drum could be heard from another room. One of the teenagers who played in the school band served as the musician.

The beat of the drum continued every eight seconds throughout the service, becoming a constant reminder of the starving people of the world. The group also projected one slide of a hungry child on the wall behind the worship center.

The group asked the people to come to the altar with their gifts for the special offering. This was done efficiently by having a youth usher stand at each row and dismiss one row at a time.

CARE

The youth group had extremely meaningful Sunday evening worship services. They felt that it was worship which really unified the teenagers from several different high schools. The worship committee had tried many different creative approaches to draw their people into an authentic relationship with God as a community of faith.

The offering was the most difficult part however. The youth had little money to give. How could they focus upon the biblical idea of stewardship through the sharing of any and all gifts? Summer vacation was coming and the members of the group would have time to give!

The team created a small booklet (three legal-size sheets, folded and stapled) for Christian offering or stewardship. They added a bit of humor by designing it Sherlock Holmes style. They set up three mysteries: time, prayer and money (things).

The team used the booklets in a journal style during the offering section of the Sunday evening service. For instance, one week they focused on solving the problem of offering one's self to others. The group thought of the following solutions: sitting for a mother with a small child, doing errands for an elderly person, cleaning up litter in parks, giving "time" gifts to your family instead of buying things, volunteering for community service projects, etc. Each person was asked to make his or her offering to God by sharing aloud what he or she would do during the next week.

After the first week of using this offering approach, the students reported on what they gave and received from God through the people they served.

GARDEN FOOD

Gardening was a major activity in the Ohio community. Everybody in the church seemed to have plots of tomatoes, peppers and other crops. The big problem was that everything ripened at the same time; there was sometimes an overabundance from the harvest.

The youth group was able to contribute an offering idea for the Sunday morning service that accomplished several goals. The teenagers had prepared several tables on the church lawn. People were encouraged to bring garden vegetables for the "offering" market. Those who needed fresh produce made a donation toward the food. The money collected was used as an offering for the hunger fund. Everyone was pleased by this opportunity to receive and give food, one of God's most wonderful gifts.

TAKING UP

An Iowa youth group held the worship service at the beginning of the Lenten season. Many traditions celebrate the practice of walking spiritually in Jesus' footsteps through observing fasting and other kinds of denial. Some people do not eat meat or desserts during the six-week period. In very strict personal disciplines, people have identified with the suffering Jesus by wearing "hair" or coarse clothing under their regular dress as their offering to God.

The group decided that the death and Resurrection of Christ also suggested added responsibility. Shouldn't the believer "take up" something as an offering? The worship team developed specific acts which would help people in their daily world. For example, they discovered that most people have problems of loneliness, anger, boredom, lack of time, fear and sadness. These moments are not necessarily crises; however, we know that they burden people. In most settings, we simply let such uncomfortable moments in other people's lives pass by.

Specific examples of helping were written on slips of paper. The teenage worship leader read Mark 8:34: "... If any man would come after me, let him deny himself and take up his cross and follow me." After spending a couple minutes in meditation on Christ's giving, each person drew a slip from the offering plate as it was passed.

Using the suggestions on the slips, the youth were asked to reflect on a specific way they could lift up the cross with another person in need. Then, the offering was made by sharing the group's plans to listen, care and help the next day.

At the next service, the youth began by sharing their acts of taking up the burden of Christ during the past week.

PERSONAL GIFTS

The confirmation class had met for several months. When the members prepared to make their public confession of faith, the pastor asked them what kind of offering they would make. What does God demand as a result of your faith commitment?

The discussion went on for several weeks. The members finally concluded that God demanded the best one could offer—whatever that was. It was decided that each person would make his or her best offering in the service. One teenager played his trumpet; a girl drew a picture which was presented to the congregation; another person wrote a poem about her relationship to Jesus; one guy actually demonstrated his expertise with a soccer ball; another member of the class outlined how he would work against war as a new disciple of Christ.

The pastor interviewed each person during the service about the particular gifts they possessed. The congregation applauded at the conclusion of this special offering experience.

PRAYERS

We have spent much time in previous chapters on creative modes of prayer. The offering is most frequently expressed by prayers of thanksgiving. God's people thank the Lord for their gifts in return. You can modify some of the ideas in that chapter for offering acts.

You also can use prayers of intercession for those who will use or receive the money gifts of offering. Intercession has been expressed by many churches in special offering acts. For example, one youth group had never been part of the traditional food drive in their church. They were actually inspired by a rock star who marked all of his concerts with a food drive for the poor and hungry. The fans carried canned food stuff to the performance.

The youth group asked for the responsibility of developing a food offering for the Advent worship services. They organized a food drive each week. At the offering time, people carried food to the front of the church. Prayers were then shared for the hungry.

TENDERNESS

A youth group in Idaho found that one of the most difficult offerings to make was gentleness. The adult leader was not sure what it was that made the teenagers so tough and critical. They often exchanged biting "humorous" remarks and put-downs. This bantering was really cruel; there was also a lot of pushing and roughness among members.

When the worship planning team focused on this problem, they realized that this dynamic could not be changed through preaching. They had to struggle with the quest to know God's gift of tenderness and love at a different point in worship.

Someone suggested that the offering might be the perfect place to celebrate a new spirit. The students gathered for a summer evening worship service. They were going to a workcamp in a few days. There would be several meetings in the next couple days.

When the time for offering came, the young person leading the service told the members of the youth group that the full offering would be delayed a week. In preparation for offering something special to God, they must use the gift.

The worshipers each were given a raw egg and told that they were entrusted with the gentle and loving care of it for the next three days. Each person also was given several pieces of paper on which to record each hour of care. Who would take care of the egg when the youth were busy with something else? How could they show gentleness to this fragile item?

The next worship experience was very interesting. The offering was the center of the whole service. Two hours were spent debriefing the events which had unfolded around the worshipers' attempt to be gentle. A few people had broken the eggs; others found that it was very difficult being responsible to something which needed constant care.

The adult adviser asked the youth to compare the treatment of the egg (with its humor and pain) to their relationship with each other. What is there about each of them that is fragile? What kind of special care has someone shown to them in the past? The youth closed with a prayer circle focusing on their offering of care and love for each other.

TALENTS

The youth group was planning the annual youth Sunday service. They joked about being inexperienced in leading the worship service. Someone suggested that was the way the rest of the congregation probably felt. We all have something special to offer God, but we all feel inexperienced.

The teenagers presented the offering by acting out six short vignettes. They used simple mime. Each situation was a human need from within the church. For instance, one scene depicted an older woman sitting in a rocking chair. Several teenage mimes showed how they were on their way to church. However the older woman could not get to church.

A couple of the scenes were touching and at least one was extremely funny. Between each scene, the group said in unison, "Can you help?"

The group asked the congregation to make their offering to God through their earnings and through a written commitment on the bulletins of their willingness to help in a specific way.

The Christian education director was delighted. She got four new teachers from this offering. A number of people were encouraged to help with the church's visitation ministry.

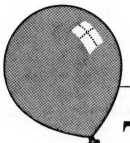

CHAPTER 12

The Sermon

In the beginning, God created all things through the Word. The Gospel of John helps us to understand the fullness of this fact. It informs us that the Word in the beginning has now become flesh and dwells among us. Thus we are given an invaluable clue to understand the relationship between the content and the experience of our faith. God has linked the spiritual and the physical for those who believe.

It is difficult for us to recognize this pivotal point of our faith when talking about God in worship. The Word has frequently been equated with only spoken words for others to hear. Those with a strong sacramental heritage have been helped by experiencing the link between the Word as the uttered truth and the Word as a mysterious sacrament. Others have been limited to the Word as only spoken words.

I do not mean to dismiss the "preaching" or homiletic mode assumed by many youth workers. The "message" part of the rally or meeting is the center of the worship experience. Many evangelical youth leaders are not comfortable without having said something. More than once, I have had conference hosts add their own sermons after the conclusion of my nontraditional experiences with the Word. They weren't willing to trust that the Spirit reached us in a nontraditional sermon form.

THE WORD BECOMES FLESH IN WORSHIP

The Word needs to be spoken in every worship event. But the worship leaders' responsibility does not end there. Speaking the Word is only the first step. An equally important question is whether the Word had been *heard* by the receivers. Have they been touched in the most private aspects of their lives? Do they truly feel the challenge of the Gospel? No method can assure a positive response to these questions. Yet, authentic proclamation of the Word requires that the *experience* of faith and the *telling* of faith are inseparable.

THE ROLE OF THE HOLY SPIRIT

My understanding of the Word in worship is rooted in another important reality: It is the Holy Spirit who makes words, actions, gestures, and thoughts become more than techniques and ideas. The presence of the Holy Spirit transforms everything. We can't control the Spirit; however, the biblical presentation of the Holy Spirit gives us clues for proclaiming the Word.

In Acts 2:1-4, we are struck by the setting for the coming of the Spirit. We are told that the community is gathered together in one place. This description is more than a detail in passing. These people have become a community of faith through the cross and the empty tomb. There is a complex and vital relationship between God working through this community and the Word which was with us in the beginning.

I understand the content of the Gospel to be Jesus Christ as revealed in the Bible. I know that adults often present moral lectures in youth worship. However, I believe the Bible is the best source for creative ideas to share the Word.

The models in this chapter are based on the Bible. My perspective differs from others because I am looking into the Bible to gain the ideas to present it. In other words, the *form* as well as the *content* of preaching emerges from the passages. You will be amazed by the way the Bible offers endless, exciting ideas for its presentation. The deeper you dig into the history, context and form of Bible passages, the more ideas you will find. Our task for preaching is to help our youth "crawl" into scripture. I am not trying to make the Bible relevant to us, but I am trying to make youth relevant to the Word.

My theological position is that the people of God are active participants in the arrival of the Word. It is true that one or more persons may be entrusted to bring the historical beginning point of the witness to Christ, but it is most important that everyone participates together in the process of the Word becoming flesh.

Does truth come from young people? Yes and no. They are not the source of the Word. The youth are limited by needs, sin, and limitations of experience and wisdom. On the other hand, if the youth have found and have been found by God, Jesus lives in them and they in him.

You will notice that our approach to the proclamation of the Word continually draws the worshipers into the process of preaching. They come to receive and share what God is doing in their midst.

RESEARCH OF THE PASSAGE IS ESSENTIAL

While I will be sharing the unique ideas from the texts themselves, do not be deceived concerning the role of research. As a former seminary lecturer in New Testament Greek and exegesis, I know that we must start with a careful study of the passage to be proclaimed. This book is not the place for a scholarly discussion of Bible passages. However, I have studied the original text and surveyed a wide range of secondary sources. You will be able to find excellent commentaries in your church library or from your pastor's personal collection. Please be sure to study the background and context of a passage under consideration.

These comments explain why my approach to presenting the Word in worship is a bit different from what you might have expected in this chapter. I will not be offering outlines or canned approaches on what one should say in a sermon. You will receive clues from the Bible to create the form for preaching.

PRESENTING THE WORD IN WORSHIP

I will offer a mini-preaching commentary on 16 different passages. I have chosen these portions of scripture at random. You will quickly absorb my approach to the proclamation part of worship. The same approach will work with any Old or New Testament material.

Don't be frustrated if I have not filled in all the spaces between the idea and the actual presentation. It would be impossible for me to assume that I could give your presentation the "flesh" it needs to meet your people.

The receivers of and participants in the Word have a very special character each time they gather. Only you and your youth can tune into this spiritual chemistry. Trust the Spirit of God working through you and the planning team. I pray that these pages will spark your youth group as you accept the burden of bearing the Word in your worship service.

GENESIS 2:7

A group of teenagers were on a workcamp. During one of the evening worship services, they experienced a particularly powerful sermon. The worship leader, Betty, read Genesis 2:7. She then passed out lumps of potter's clay to each member of the crew.

Betty described one of the poor families whom they had met in their workcamp. The lady had six children and no money; their life was very desperate.

Betty asked each of the youth to take the perspective of someone involved in the story of this poor family: hungry children, mother, neighbor, social worker, husband who left, etc. The worshipers were guided to view the story from their particular perspective.

Betty then asked the youth to shape their clay in such a way that their assigned perspective on life would be most clearly presented. These constructions were then discussed. There was a very strong exchange of ideas and insights.

After a few minutes, Betty asked the young people to look at the situation from God's perspective. She reread the verse. The members then shared how God looks upon this poor family. This moving sermon experience helped the youth to understand the purpose of the workcamp.

JOSHUA 24:1-28

This stirring convenant between God and the tribes of

Israel touches all of us. Each person needs to make a choice. The Lord is known in the saving acts of history: One will either serve the Lord or some other god.

For the person presenting a sermon on this passage, there are at least five basic points in this story which come from the page: prologue (what the Lord God has done in the past), the stipulations (conditions of the covenant), the actual oath (we will serve the Lord), the ceremony of the covenant, the witness to the act ("this stone shall be a witness").

Covenant acts in the Bible have symbols to remind people of what they promise with their hearts and minds. These symbols are similar to the wedding rings couples often choose to pledge their faithfulness to each other. God knows that we are limited as creatures; the incarnation of the Word in Jesus Christ is the single most important factor enabling us to touch, taste, see, hear and feel the truth.

When I presented a sermon from this passage for a congregation of teenagers, I offered a series of "signs," which promised things (toothpaste—a bright smile, shampoo—shiny hair, etc.).

I then produced a stone that was long and wide, but thin so that it was manageable. I told the story of Joshua. I held the stone over my head when I came to Joshua's famous line, "... but as for me and my house, we will serve the Lord" (Joshua 24:15).

Since there were only 25 worshipers, I passed the stone to each of them. I asked each person to relate the emotions which this memorial stone overheard that day.

I passed the stone around again and asked each person to share an experience of making a promise before God and perhaps others at some time in his or her life. I told the youth that they also could share moments of a covenant oath they had not yet faced (marriage, court, etc.).

I organized the worshipers into five groups and assigned each one a part of the ceremony of covenant. I asked the groups to create a way by which this body could repeat this covenant. I wrote the five points about the covenant on a posted piece of newsprint.

We reconvened after about five minutes. The conclusion of the proclamation was a reenactment of the passage in our own setting. Each cluster of worshipers led us through its assigned part of the ceremony; the stone was the concluding act. The stone remained part of our worship centerpiece for the remainder of the year.

ECCLESIASTES 3:1-9

When I was on a teaching tour of Australia, a television producer halted our conversation by suggesting, "Let's wait a tick." It took a moment to realize that his expression was similar to the North American phrase, "Wait a minute." Time is an amazing concept. We use time to portray the span of our lives.

Ecclesiastes 3 is one of the most disturbing statements concerning the perspective one needs about time. There is a sadness and a joy in the quality of time's focus.

We were sitting in a grove of trees at a retreat setting in Michigan. I passed around a windup alarm clock. I had only read and discussed a few verses when the alarm went off. (I had set it so it would do this.)

I stopped my reading and asked the shocked person who was holding the clock to share an incident from her life when time seemed to stand still. I encouraged that person to pass the clock on to the next person. I suggested that the person listen to the ticking and reflect on the passing of time. I asked the next person to report on a moment when he did not want time to change. After we had circled the worshipers with this kind of sharing, I read the passage.

I divided the youth into pairs and gave each team one of the verses. I encouraged them to decide which side of the "tick" they would embrace most joyfully. When we started sharing the stories inspired by the verses, I was amazed by how many teenagers felt trapped between the two sides of each moment in time.

We closed with the affirmation that God was Lord over all times. We are given the capability to embrace both sides of the time line. We closed the sermon with a silent prayer. I passed the clock once again and let everyone listen to the flight of time.

ISAIAH 53:1-12

This passage stings and bites into the deepest levels of

caring and emotion. The innocent one takes upon himself the bruises and punishing blows of the guilty. This teaching forces us to look at our lives from a different perspective. The Messiah does not come forth as a majestic hero. The Lamb of God will be found in the most unlikely form. This teaching, as seen from the perspective of the New Testament, forces us to look at those around us with a different set of standards than the most popular people in the world. The passage beckons the believer to walk in the steps of the rejected and uncomely in the quest for the Savior.

At a youth worship, I led a devotion by using bruised lemons as the parabolic focus. (You could use another familiar fruit that is slightly spoiled or deformed.) The fruit should be something that is very familiar and overlooked in value by the worshipers.

Choose a single slide of a well-dressed person or a hungry child. Leave the image on the bare wall of the worship area; you don't need fancy equipment or even a screen. You also can project the image in a lighted room. The participants only need to be able to see the person.

Read the passage and ask each person to describe what ways the person affirms or challenges the message. Pass around the bruised lemon and have the students tell how this fruit says something about the suffering servant in the text. Allow the students to reflect on their own ideas. They will do well in lifting up the teachings of the sermon.

Move the youth more personally into the passage by asking them how their lives relate to the teaching. For example, "If you were the person on the screen, how would life support or challenge the teaching that the Messiah comes to us through the poor and suffering?"

Pick up the clue of the physical bruises on the fruit. Give each person a bandage to wear on his or her hand as a reminder to look to the needy for salvation.

The sensual images of the root torn from the ground also can be utilized. Follow the preceding outline by using a dry root instead of the bruised piece of fruit. If you can find fruit which smells badly, you easily can compare our deodorized culture to the uncomeliness of this source of our salvation.

You will be amazed how easily the major points of the passage's teaching will emerge from the people: The Gospel will arise within the community of faith.

MARK 1:21-31

This passage reports the public response to the power of Jesus. One planning team wanted to explore this kind of power in contrast to the phony models of power in our world of stars (sports, music, politics, etc.).

The team members found large poster-size cutout shapes of several contemporary heroes. At the sermon time, the worship leader, Jim, showed these pictures and asked the worshipers to list the characteristics that gave the heroes so much popularity.

The leader then turned the cutout over so that the blank cardboard faced the worshipers. The passage was then read.

The teenagers were asked to share the qualities which made people realize that Jesus has power. Jim wrote these on the cardboard and had the students compare the qualities.

MARK 15:21-37

Paul and his youth group planned a most interesting sermon as part of their Good Friday service. The service was sponsored by several churches in this small Georgia town. It took the form of an actual parade through the middle of the community. The youth were dressed as Roman soldiers, Jesus, the thieves and others. The high school drama people were most helpful in terms of providing costumes and makeup. This pageant moved through town and ended in a church sanctuary. The actors froze in a Crucifixion setting with the soldiers gambling at the foot of the cross for Jesus' garment.

A teenage worship leader took the role of a reporter and came down the aisle with a microphone; she slowly and completely described the scene. The basic emotions affecting each group at the cross were outlined.

After her description of the gambling soldiers, she faced the worshipers and challenged them with the question, "What games do we play with Christ's suffering?"

The youth then distributed a dice to each worshiper. The congregation was asked to reflect on the answer to that question for their lives. The background music was "Were You There When They Crucified My Lord?"

After a few minutes, the leader asked if the worshipers wanted to share the reflections which came to them as they reflected on this biblical scene. She and several other teenagers quickly moved around the worshipers with microphones for their responses.

Each worshiper was asked to take the dice with him or her as a reminder of the price Christ paid on the cross to set us free of all sin.

LUKE 9:23

Jesus states the cost of discipleship quite clearly and strongly. If a person is to follow the Lord, he or she must carry the cross daily and follow his path.

This passage speaks to many of us who pursue a comfortable faith. Ironically, the sect groups usually demand more from their disciples than most youth groups. We often try to win youth with entertainment and easy solutions to difficult problems. Young people need a faith which demands discipline.

The cross creates many interesting ideas for the sermon. Joe, a youth leader, and the worship planning team took this passage and let different kinds of crosses create the dynamics of the message. After a bit of preparation, the time for the Word opened with the reading of the passage.

Joe started talking about the cross in the life of Christ. One of the youth then showed his cross. It was padded with fine material. The youth said that his cross was a comfortable cross; he could lean on it and rest.

Another person presented her "designer" cross. It had a little alligator sewed in the center.

The next person shared a bulky cross which had "muscles" on the crossbars. This "macho" cross was for tough guys.

Another young person searched in his pocket to find a small polished cross. He kept it hidden until he needed it.

Each of the students went to a different corner of the room after presenting his or her cross. Joe asked the other students to go to the cross which best represented themselves.

He reread the passage and then asked the youth to share in their groups how their respective crosses related to what Jesus was saying.

After a few minutes, Joe called the students to attention. A teenager brought in a simple wooden cross. This "old rugged" cross was like the one in scripture—simple, painful, demanding and liberating. Joe reread the passage.

He asked the students to share how this cross did not fit the witness the students had to make each day in following Jesus. Marvelous insights into the challenge of discipleship were revealed in their comments. Joe suggested that the real cross of Jesus was actually within each of the youth.

The sermon was concluded by having the group form a circle. Joe and the other worship leaders went around the group and made the outline of a cross on the back of each person.

JOHN 8:31-38

Jesus was a refugee. He was carried forth from his home while he was still in his mother's womb. In this passage, the listeners are refugees from their spiritual heritage. Jesus offers them a home in his Word, but they refuse to enter.

Give your young worshipers a feeling for this sense of spiritual dislocation by physically relocating them. Gather about 20 of the worshipers into a small square at the center of the worship area.

Make a slight platform of wood or tape off a section with masking tape to represent a raft of boat people. Allow just enough room for the youth to stand. Read the passage and talk a bit about it while these people are standing in this crowded space.

Have the participants imagine that they are forced to

leave their lands and seek another home. What will be difficult to leave behind? What is fearful ahead?

Ask the people to be seated along the edge of the platform. Talk with them about the experience of being crowded and leaving home. What will be difficult about resettlement? Tell them that this group has been offered some land in a rural part of the country. The refugees want a new start; however, the people who live in this area do not want them there. How would the congregation respond?

Close the sermon by having people in the pews go one at a time and bring a "boat person" back to the pew.

JOHN 18:15-18, 25-27

This dramatic scene touches each of us. We all know how it feels to deny Christ. Peter is caught in the crosswinds of conflicting emotions. He loves Jesus yet lacks the courage to stand with him in a time of trial.

This passage begs for a dramatic presentation. In the worship center, place newspaper on the floor. Pile charcoal onto the newspaper to represent the fire which is the focal point of the story.

Ask several students to imagine the stories the fire could tell about a similar situation. These need to be spoken and not read. For example:

1. A Nazi soldier: "I am a member of the German state church. When the Fuhrer came to power in 1934, many of us in the church were glad that someone had finally attempted to reconstruct the Germans' morals. We have learned to support the National Socialist reorganization of the church to better serve Christian morals. You know, Herr Hitler does not smoke!"

2. An alcoholic or drug abuser: "This whole world is a bunch of garbage, ya know! I work myself to the bone to pay my bills, feed my family, educate my children. For what? It is so cold out there. I get my warmth from this (holds up drink)."

3. A pew warmer: "I think that it is nice to go to church. It is so holy. The stained-glass windows, the candles on the altar, and the neat rows of pews with my own reserved seat give me a warm feeling. Nothing

changes and it is so comfortable!''

Explore the use of costumes and gestures. The characters should represent a variety of people who have let themselves succumb to a destructive flame.

After a character finishes a vignette, have him or her sit with you around the fire. After all scenes are done, take some of the charcoal and pass it around the group with the blessing that God is the only source of light. He will protect us from the cold and burn away our failures and sins.

Include the worshipers by asking them to reflect on their inner raging fires. Bless them with the same assurance you shared with the characters. Hold the charcoal over the heads of the congregation as you offer the closing words of the sermon.

JOHN 20:1-18

Before the service, ask the youth to collect one small stone for each worshiper. Invite a stone polisher in the church or community to give you support in this matter. Such a skilled person can polish the simplest stone to its true beauty.

Distribute one stone to each worshiper and invite the participants to reflect on it. If that stone had been at the tomb on that dark morning, what would it have to tell us? Encourage the worshipers to share the story from this perspective. Another way to deliver the sermon is to tell the story from the perspective of the stone each person is holding. If it were looking at the congregation at this service, what would it see about our attitudes? It is amazing how direct a third-party perspective can be.

Let the stone describe the characters as persons caught in the crosswinds of the past and future. Invite the worshipers to share what their Resurrection stones say about the problems of today.

Another way to deliver the sermon is to place a large rock in the middle of the worship area. Ask the youth to imagine they are in the garden at the time of Jesus' Resurrection.

Close the sermon by holding the large rock over your head. Ask the students to do the same with their smaller stones. Say, ''May the Resurrection stone be a memorial to what God has done for us in Jesus Christ."

JOHN 21:1-14

The fishing net is a helpful image when presenting your sermon. Explore the kinds of fishing nets available in your area. Try to find a rugged one. If you live near the sea, collect seashells or seaweed.

The net was used by people who fished at the time of the New Testament. There were even gladiator events that featured the net. For many Christians, the net became the symbol of evangelism (see Matthew 4:19 and parallels).

In the worship center, place the net at the base of the cross or drape the net over the cross. Have some young people use offering plates to distribute the shells to the congregation.

Suggest that God calls us to cast our nets into the sea of our culture. Each person caught in the net of the Gospel is special.

Have each worshiper reflect on his or her shell. Who are some of the people who need to be gathered into the net of faith? Ask some of the youth to call out the names of those who have this need.

Ask several young people to come and stretch the net. How strong is it? Share the tensions which have always raged within the faith community. Collect the shells in the net and ask how much the net of faith can hold in terms of controversy. Have the teenagers offer suggestions about the strains in the net of faith.

Don't feel that you have to do battle over disagreements within your faith community. You are an instrument of the Gospel; it is your task to transform the energy into love.

ACTS 9:10-19

At a youth gathering, the closing worship service was totally designed by the 150 participants. One cluster of young people came up with an exciting way to present the sermon.

They had been assigned this famous passage in Acts. This story takes place after Paul has been confronted by the Spirit on the road. The scene shifts to a faithful Christian in the nearby city. Ananias ends up in a debate with the Spirit in which Ananias refuses to let the message of God move through his spiritual blindness.

The teenagers utilized mime and dialogue to present the outlines of the story. They were able to find simple mime roles for many of their group. For example, different people were assigned characters in the passage, foot stomping was used for thunder, hand clapping was used for galloping horses, etc. There was a great deal of laughter as the youth reacted to this simple but expressive form of communication.

A teenager took a microphone with him out of the room. He spoke deeply and used the microphone to imitate the voice of the angel. It was incredibly effective.

Ananias struggled with what a faithful person "knows" is right from experience and what is right when the Spirit speaks. I could feel a chill running up my spine as Ananias came to "see" spiritually as he healed Paul physically.

ACTS 9:10-19 (again)

Almost 1,500 teenagers were at a Kansas youth conference. I did not want to fall into the usual preaching format with this group. It was my hope that they could share their struggles with this passage. How does one involve 1,500 people in a preaching activity?

I opened by wearing my body screen. This is actually a large white robe which stretches out to a 5-foot-by-6-foot screen when I hold my arms out straight. It was made by a friend from scrap materials. You can make one by taking a large piece of cloth and cutting a hole in the center for your head; this becomes a poncho.

Teenagers directed images onto my body from two movie projectors. The images were of people in need, (sick, hungry, etc.) taken from an old stewardship film.

After hearing the story and visualizing the message of passage. I shared an account of my stay in the hospital for polio. Other people helped me heal through touch and acceptance.

I then asked the mass of young people to choose a person next to them. I asked the pairs to take turns putting both hands on the face of the other. I led them through the actual words of verse 17: "Brother/sister ____(Name)____, the Lord Jesus ... has sent me that you may regain your sight and be filled with the Holy Spirit."

I asked the youth to step forward and tell how God healed them through loving people. There were 60 seconds of silence; I wondered if anyone would speak to the passage from their experience. Then the first young person came to the microphone in the aisle. She told us how the prayer of loving friends and family had helped her in her battle with cancer.

Another young man shared his fearful experience of breaking his neck. This tough guy started crying as he told about the love and care of those who prayed for him. I hugged him; the whole congregation of teenagers stood and applauded. The healing of Paul and Ananias was made known in our presence.

ACTS 23:11-15

Paul speaks to a divided house; however, he doesn't back away from the conflicts which emerge. Forty zealous opponents of the apostle vow that they will not eat or drink until they have killed him.

This passage suggests a number of exciting ideas for a sermon setting. Gather a number of symbols which are used to mark a vow. For example, a stone (convenant of Joshua), ring (wedding), knife (blood kinship), headband with design (World War II Japanese suicide pilots). Note that vows can be centered around life or death.

Read the passage and pass around the symbols. Ask each person to give an example of the contrasts between a covenant of hope and a covenant of death.

Elaborate on the image of the death vow being sealed with fasting (Acts 23:14). Remember how this vow of revenge works against the vow of Jesus as he served the bread and cup.

Serve a love feast of bread and juice. There are various traditions which treat a Lord's Supper differently. Most people have no problem with a love feast where a vow of love and hope can be renewed and celebrated. Say that Jesus promised that as often as we eat and drink, he would be with us.

This would be an excellent passage to use as sermon material for a pre-Easter service. Students could vow to help someone, rather than focus on giving up something.

ACTS 25:1-12

This passage is rich in dialogue. We are given numerous perspectives as the message unfolds.

Copy this passage and use a pencil to outline the actual speeches. When the sermon time begins, divide the worshipers into several groups. You or a youth group member take the transitions ("and Paul said ..." statements). Divide the congregation into groups and assign each group a character in the story. Have the congregation repeat the speeches of the characters in the passage.

The nice thing about using the passage's own message is that you can actually practice reading it in this manner with the congregation. If you want to follow the dialogue format of the text, place the preaching "moments" between each of the readings. This will give the passage a type of a litany. The modern broadcast world has discovered this ancient technique. The commercial has emerged as the single most influential television format. The Bible and the church have realized this for a long time, but failed to skillfully use its heritage.

You will be amazed at how much impact can be generated by dropping 90 seconds of sermon every few minutes.

ACTS 27:1-44

The passage is a wonderfully dramatic presentation of God's work in the life of Paul. He is sailing to Rome for the last part of his life. The scene would make a fine movie script as well as a dramatic form for a sermon.

You might want to record a sea storm from a sound-effects record. Use a cassette recorder and borrow the record from your public library.

The ship is one of the most basic Christian symbols. Borrow an anchor from someone in the community or have a person in the church make one out of wood.

Begin the sermon by having someone suggest that this

anchor was part of the ship carrying Paul on his journey. Keeping the lights low, play the sounds of the storm. Have the anchor tell the story of the passage. How are the different people on the ship handling the situation?

Pass the anchor around and have each worshiper share the feelings to which he or she can most easily relate. What do they think about those who would give up or won't take advice from Paul?

You will be surprised by the impact this inside perspective of the passage gives to this kind of presentation.

ACTS 27:1-44 (again)

The people in this passage had to make important decisions about life and death. Drawing the congregation into the process of this passage will make an excellent sermon.

Print the following sentences on the back of the bulletin or on a slip of paper if it is a small group of worshipers.

1. If I had been the centurion, I would have _____
2. If I had been Paul and knew all the bad things that were going to happen, I would have _____.
3. I feel like the centurion when _____.
4. I wish I had the confidence of Paul when _____.

Feel free to create other role statements which will better fit your group.

Recount the content of the passage using a storytelling approach. Tell the story without using any notes. Then ask the worshipers to complete the sentences.

Have the worshipers share their answers to the last two questions. If you are leading a youth service with many worshipers, just place microphones in each of the aisles.

Don't view such an open sermon format as a mere sharing of ignorance. The blend of your team's preparation and the way God touches the worshiper is a perfect match.

ACTS 27:1-44 (once more)

This rich passage recalls a historical journey. It also communicates the spiritual teaching of how God sustains those who believe in him. Indeed, Luke is showing us that

God's preservation of Paul demonstrates the apostle's innocence.

Offer the sermon by inviting the congregation to discover the parallel between the flow of their lives and Paul's trip.

Present several symbols which reflect aspects of the story (a rope, pile of grain, sword, plank of driftwood, chains, etc.). As you present each symbol and part of the story, have members of the planning team draw a parallel to contemporary life. The person sharing can invite other worshipers to offer their contributions. For example, what is the cargo (grain) which must be cast overboard in our lives during difficult times? What would you throw away?

You also could distribute one of the symbols to the worshipers as a reminder of Paul's story when they face difficult times; for instance, distribute small pieces of driftwood. In advance, prepare these symbols by cutting an old piece of weathered wood into small sections.

ACTS 27:1-44 (the last time around)

The conclusion of this story is near. The soldiers plan to kill the prisoners to protect themselves from the charge of letting them escape. The centurion diverts the intention of the troops and the prisoners are able to make their way to the shore on planks or pieces of the ship.

Present the sermon from the perspective of that dramatic moment of rescue. Place a large plank on two sawhorses. Have the person leading the sermon sit on the plank as if he or she were holding onto it for survival.

Play a recording of a stormy sea. Have the person tell the story of the shipwreck while asking the worshipers to close their eyes and imagine that they also are set adrift with Paul and the others.

Move the story into the present. What are the stormy seas of our lives? Ask the youth to feel the bouncing waves and the howling wind. Have them hold onto the pews for security. What are the things onto which we can hold during these stormy times? Encourage the young people to share their responses to this application of the passage. Give each person a piece of driftwood as a reminder that Christ is with them always.

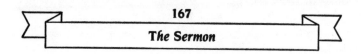

1 CORINTHIANS 12:12-27

The youth group was on a workcamp trip. On the way to the site, they stopped at the beach. It was a meaningful time of celebration. As the sun was going down, they gathered for worship.

At the sermon portion of the service, Tom, the teenage leader, read 1 Corinthians 12:12-27. He asked the worshipers to spend a couple minutes on the beach in silence. He invited them to find something which explained the teaching of this passage.

Another young person played the guitar softly as the group wandered on the shore. Tom then gathered the group in a circle around a fire. Each person presented his or her item from the beach and shared how it related to the teaching about how important each part of the body is. For example, one person found a beautiful shell . She said, "No matter if it were beautiful or not so beautiful, God loves us and we are special."

Tom then read the verses and asked the youth to form a giant body by stretching out on the sand. As he called out parts from the text, people found places in the sand and actually became the connected body of faith.

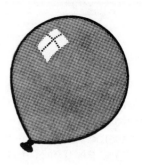

CHAPTER 13

The Commissioning

Parting is always painful. It is particularly difficult for God's people to say farewell to the worship experience and the fellowship of the faith community. As the service ends, we are forced to break our physical communion with God and our sisters and brothers.

We know that we will not be together in this particular gathering until we meet again in the kingdom of God. The Messianic community becomes only a memory as we break ranks and go our separate ways. This knowledge brings both sadness and joy.

The scattering of the people at the end of worship is also an uncomfortable moment because we know that we must now face the loneliness of our individual witness in a hostile world. The Christian is really a wayfarer on a journey. From time to time, he or she stops along the way for spiritual nurture with other travelers. The worship experience is the gathering of kindred spirits to draw upon the warmth of God's hospitality. It is difficult to break this circle of hope and face the cold, hard trail.

THE CHARGE

When we plunge out into the world on our own, it is God who sends us with a blessing and a charge. In a sense, God kicks us out of this comfortable nesting moment with the commission to be the body of Christ among others who do not know the Lord.

In the moment of the Transfiguration (Matthew

17:1-13), we find the favored disciples in the presence of the transfigured Lord and the visiting prophets. These early followers yearned to freeze this moment by building booths to frame the emotional excitement of such a spiritual revelation. But Jesus did not allow for attempts to cling to temporary moments. He told them to leave the mountaintop inspiration in order to heal a man's son.

Youth groups often have difficulty in celebrating mountaintop experiences. Young people are asked to make commitments that are often life changing. But the excitement of commitment must be left on the "mountaintop" and replaced with a disciple's lifestyle.

THE ALTAR CALL

Many traditions conclude worship with a moment of commitment. This can range from words of blessing to a call for people to come up front and give their lives to Christ. Many mainline churches have stayed away from these regular calls for faith commitment. However, I believe that both the altar call and the words of benediction are important and need to be included in the commissioning. We are sent from worship to assume our discipleship. It is vital to celebrate this reality in our worship experience.

The public acknowledgment of commissioning can come at any place in the worship service. In the following examples, it is possible to utilize the commissioning clues at places other than the conclusion of the worship. I will bring up special opportunities for this aspect of worship which may not be ordinarily considered by youth groups.

THE NEW DRIVER

Passage points are some of the most influential moments of our Christian lives. These are the times when the community and the individual suddenly receive a very different perspective on a person's life. Experiences such as graduating from high school, getting married, winning the first job are all quite emotional in nature.

It is important that the faith community celebrates these striking moments of change in the lives of the young and old. The passage moments are connection points at which the Gospel touches the lives of believers. It is important that the believer links such changes and opportunities to God's abiding love and presence.

There was a day when the young could win respect and confidence by driving the team of horses in the field. The rifle, the first acceptable handmade quilt or other accomplishments marked that the child had become an adult. For contemporary young people, the winning of a driver's license is probably the most important maturation signpost. Traditionally, the church has not noted this moment. The freedom to drive means that the young person is now free to go wherever he or she wants. Sometimes this mobility permits the young person to stay away from church!

At least one pastor is sensitive to this dynamic. Ed has created a short liturgical moment for the Sunday service in which teenagers are commissioned to the responsibility of driving. The young person who has passed the driver's test is invited to come forward. The person kneels while several people surround him or her.

Ed invites the parents and other significant adults to join them. The adults place their hands on the young person's head and commission the new driver. Ed focuses his prayer on thanksgiving for bringing this person to the age of responsibility.

They then give the young person a key chain with a small cross on it. The pastor charges the youth to let this symbol remind him or her that this congregation loves and supports him or her at all times. No matter what temptation may face the student or how dangerous a situation may seem, he or she can be confident that the love and prayers of the congregation are present.

The teenager then stands at the door of the church and receives the greetings from the worshipers. Ed notes that it is important not to undertake this type of commissioning with more than one young person per service. The young person deserves and needs a personal focus of prayer and love at this important passage point. The church tends to "broom" people through passage moments and perform mass passage celebrations. Yet, each time we undertake this kind of worship moment, we are actually glorifying God's work through our brothers and sisters. There is always time in worship for such moments.

YOUTH GROUP OFFICERS

Worship is the place for commissioning the people chosen to lead the youth group. If you are a youth adviser, you may think that getting officers is a chore. Yet, there is something quite special about being chosen to provide leadership in ministry. If there is low priority among your teenagers to hold office in your group, it may indicate that officers don't really do anything. Such an attitude also may indicate that they aren't valued by adult leadership and the church.

Rituals of commissioning demand carefully chosen language. Select a youth team and write the vows for new officers and members of the group. You might alter the promises which are used in your church for adults.

If you don't have such written promises, you will need to consider five partners in this commissioning act: the officers elect; the former officers; the members of the group; the adult congregation; and God.

Each of these segments of the faith family will need to be included in your commissioning ritual. Write a simple sentence which draws upon their willingness to be part of this convenant. For example, the sentence for officers may read like this: "I (name) vow before God to accept the responsibilities of leading this fellowship in glorifying God."

The members will pledge their willingness to accept this leadership. The adult church will vow to support and respect the youth leaders. The whole covenant is undertaken with God as witness and protector. Lift up a biblical passage such as Joshua 24 to give the sense of covenant to the commissioning moment.

The former leaders also have something important to contribute. Take the time to celebrate the gift of their past leadership. It is important to create symbols of office and use them in the service. The symbols could be T-shirts, hats, crosses or something which will focus on the office. One pastor, for example, installed adult officers by giving each person a key to the church.

The perfect setting for this part of worship would be

the Sunday morning service so that the congregation could affirm the young people.

YOUTH WHO ARE PARTING

In every church, young people leave to follow the course of their lives. They journey away from the home church for college, military service, a new job or the relocation of their family. Sometimes the young depart for a particular task such as a workcamp, vacation or overseas mission. All of these separations are significant in terms of worship. It is important to celebrate them in the worship of God by the people of faith.

A few years ago I traveled with a major rock-and-roll band on a radio interview assignment. I was deeply moved by our parting moments. It had only been a week that I shared their hospitality as we swept across the country; yet the leader of the band put a gold medallion around my neck at that last meeting. "Dennis, you have been a member of our family. I want you to wear this token of the tour as a symbol of our times together." I was nearly in tears as I hugged this crazy rock-and-roll crew. My real sadness was for the church. We have much better reasons for missing our brothers and sisters, but we don't know how to celebrate their departure.

Parting from your circle of friends is particularly difficult for young people. This passage point can be celebrated in a number of ways at the worship service. For instance, one youth group in Idaho has developed a special worship segment which focuses on a member who is leaving. The teenagers stand in a circle and lay their hands on the head of the kneeling member. The prayer circle focuses on affirming what the person means to them. They then present a small cross to the person. One of the special aspects of this worship act is that they systematically write letters to the person over a period of several weeks.

THOSE WHO GO TO SERVE

It is vital that the whole congregation celebrates in worship the commissioning of those who depart from the community in order to serve. Many churches have been excellent in sending their youth on service projects with a special time in worship. The Sunday morning worship service is the best setting for this type of commissioning.

One small church in Delaware has created a liturgical ritual by which the young people are commissioned in worship. Congregational members agree to pray for specific young members of the work team during a certain time of day while the youth are away. These prayer sponsors stand behind their designated student during the commissioning. These moments become very moving and meaningful for all involved. This type of commissioning does a great deal to help adults understand the special contribution youth make to the life of the church.

You also can use the amplified phone as a way for the youth to share their work. During the worship service, a phone call is placed to the youth. The conversation is amplified so the entire congregation can hear it.

THOSE WHO WORSHIP

Church worship often ends up being an end in itself. We have said that worship focuses on glorifying God. However, it is not an escape from the world. Every encounter with God sharpens our responsibility to be faithful in other parts of our lives. These thoughts suggest that the altar call or commitment is important for contemporary worship.

A church in California ends every youth worship with a specific opportunity for service. For instance, the preaching acts might focus on hunger. When the time for parting comes, the worshiping youth are asked to gather for a few minutes to consider a direct service opportunity in the food pantry for hungry people in the community. Not every young person will pick up the challenge. The youth leader, George, has found that the young people in the church have continually accepted these opportunities as an act of responding to the Gospel.

It is surprising how specific ways of living the Gospel can be found when commissioning is taken seriously. My wife's most disturbing response to my preaching is "so what?" In other words, how does the message of worship touch how we are going to live in the minutes after the benediction? Every worshiper has the right and responsibility to ask this question. Christians aren't left with a sense of helplessness upon hearing the Word. Christ calls us to discipleship at every worship.

THE COMMUNITY

The final blessing at the conclusion of worship is the moment of affirmation concerning God's presence in our journey of faith. In most Christian celebrations, this prayer is offered by the pastor who draws upon the scripture for his or her words.

How do we help young people experience the reality of this presence? Some groups offer the blessing by passing it from one person to another. The youth lock arms, form a tight circle and repeat a phrase such as, "May God watch between me and you while we are apart from one another." Hugging is also a favorite way to express the "holy kiss" (1 Corinthians 16:20).

Leonard Nimoy, Mr. Spock of "Star Trek," told about the origin of the Vulcan greeting and parting used in the show (hand held upright with the last small fingers held together and the other two held together). He adapted it from the Hebrew letter *sheen*. This letter of the alphabet stands for shalom (peace).

Leonard Nimoy told about a time when he was a young boy in school. At the end of the day, his rabbi had the students face the back of the meeting place which symbolized the world they were about to enter again. The rabbi held both hands over the heads of the people in position to represent the Hebrew letter.

This idea could be recycled by your youth. Have them offer such a blessing over the heads of each other.

Reverse the call to worship idea shared in an earlier chapter and call each person by name "out of the service." Do this by having someone call the names from outside the room.

For special meaning, give each person a symbol of the commissioning. Every covenant ceremony in the Old Testament utilizes an object by which the people who make the promise can be helped to remember the significance of the act. Use symbols such as stones, crosses, candles, etc.

NEW MEMBERS

One of the important passage rites for Christians is the public confession of faith. This is a vital moment, whether your church practices a membership system which is based purely on the movement of the Spirit or an intentional confirmation process.

Many churches offer a series of courses and then finalize the membership process at a worship service. After a public confession of faith, the congregation can give each student a cross or some other symbol to mark the day.

One church has developed an exciting commissioning moment at this key event in the lives of teenagers. They give each person a simple silver ring. It is one of the most basic symbols for the covenant relationship and can be worn for a lifetime. While the rings cost a bit more than the usual cross, this is a very meaningful act. A local jewelry maker produces the rings and the church has the date of the commissioning inscribed inside.

A meaningful symbol for those confessing their faith in Christ can take many forms. A kinship bracelet was used by another church. One of the confirmation classes designed a coat of arms to express how Christ touched them as part of the class. The bracelets were inscribed with the coat of arms. During the service, each person was presented with the bracelet.

THOSE FACING NEW WORK

I was leading a worship experience at a military base for young soldiers. They had finished their special training and were to go to new assignments all over the world after our closing worship service.

The sense of commissioning and benediction was important for this scattering community. I learned that there was a strong mixture of feelings in the midst of the group. Some were unhappy with their assignments; others were happy to get what they wanted; everyone was tense over the general unknown future. We had enjoyed our time together and there was a certain sadness over the dissolution of our community.

I told a story about a rabbit which gave its life for

others (**Barrington Bunny** by Martin Bell). During this time, I passed around a rabbit skin. By the time I came to the blessing section of the service, everyone was in tears. I asked each person to choose another for the act of blessing. I encouraged the soldiers to put their hands on the shoulders of another as an act of blessing. It was a very powerful moment; we could feel the Spirit in our midst. All the barriers of disappointment, fear and joy were removed. We could celebrate the glory of God as we said farewell to each other.

The combination of any story which evokes our own feelings with the opportunity to bless each other is very meaningful. You easily can use these clues in the moments which find your group departing for the summer or the graduation of seniors. Don't overlook the use of touch to communicate the blessing of God to your youth group.

THE STRANGER

I was in an Australian town for several days. At the end of the event, the 100 marvelous young people piled into cars and escorted me to the airport. They then led me through a touching benediction.

The young people formed a long human arch by pairing, facing each other and holding hands. This created a long "London Bridge Is Falling Down" type of tunnel. They began singing and urged me to walk under this arch of human hands.

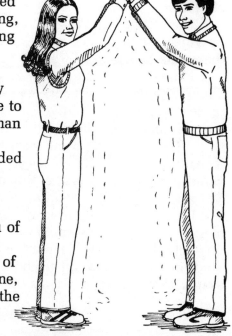

The young people crowded around me and gave me a boomerang which had been inscribed, "To our brother Dennis. May this assure you of coming back soon."

When I reached the top of the external steps to the plane, I turned around and waved the toy light sword (from my "Star Wars" event) over my head. The lighted prop stood out in the late evening dusk. A huge cheer arose from the 100 teenagers at the gate.

These people suggested some very important clues concerning the final blessing for those who must leave the youth group. The community ritual of forming the human bridge and singing a farewell is very powerful. The parting gift which reminds the person of future return is also an excellent idea for your group.

THE TEAM

Some people get uncomfortable when they hear that the professional football team has a chaplain. People are even unhappy when they receive reports about those churches which bless animals or cars. Yet, these interesting examples underscore the fact that God is Lord over all. Is it wrong for the faithful to celebrate this relationship in worship? Often these moments are special services; yet, they also appear in the midst of regular worship experiences.

One church in Indiana had several members of the local basketball team in the youth group. It was decided by the youth group officers that they would invite the whole team to the youth group the week before the big state play-off game.

The worship team designed a special worship service in which the town's concern for the big game was part of the whole experience. When it came to the time for commissioning, the worshipers were asked to form a large circle. The worship leader, Jean, held up a basketball. She passed it around the circle and asked each person to share one blessing he or she would ask God to grant for the team. The surprising thing was, the young people did not focus on winning! There was a real sensitivity to other values which would play a part in this forthcoming event. There were many prayers for the other team.

Jean found that the players were deeply moved by this blessing from their peers. What special sports or community activities are the main interests of your youth? What kinds of blessings do those about to take college entrance exams need? These moments are fitting for worship.

A PEACE WORKER

Brian's family really didn't understand. Why would a good student drop out of college for a year and walk around the world for peace? Many of the adults in church could not get excited about this strange journey. Yet, this is what Brian felt called to do by his relationship with Jesus.

He knew that the next 12 months would be filled with uncertainty. Brian and a small group of other students were not even sure that they would be permitted to enter some countries. In fact, they hadn't even raised money for the journey. Yet, they all felt that Christ was leading them on this trek of faith.

The youth group at Brian's home church had been a very important part of his development as a Christian. When the youth group members heard that Brian would soon be leaving for this trek for peace, they wanted to send him on his way with a special blessing.

The group invited Brian to the evening worship service. For the commissioning and blessing, the members invited Brian to sit in a chair which had been placed at the center of their worship circle. They removed his shoes and took turns washing his feet. Then they anointed Brian's feet with lotion. All of the youth put their hands on his head and shoulders and prayed for him.

The youth group members gave Brian a cassette tape recorder and charged him to keep an audio diary so that they might share in his wandering journey for peace.

You may not have anyone taking such a faith sojourn; however, there are youth everywhere who feel called to make special acts of discipleship. These moments when young people respond to the Spirit need to be celebrated in worship.

THE CHRISTMAS PEOPLE

One congregation in Australia finds special joy in Christmas Eve services. They have found that people are prepared to share in ways which are simply not considered at other times.

One year the congregation involved the youth in designing the service. The story of those who followed the star (shepherds, wisemen, the holy family in flight) was the biblical focus. The youth group members went to a stationery supply store and purchased little stars with adhesive backing.

During the service, the president of the youth group informed the worshipers that a "Christ Star" would be given by youth to each person as he or she left the building. The people were urged to wear them on their hands or watches until the next Sunday service. The student told the worshipers that at that time they would have an opportunity to share the experiences they had had as others asked about the Christ Star.

At the end of the service, the youth group members were at the doors of the church. They placed a small star on the hand, forehead or watches of the worshipers. They blessed each person with the benediction, "May the Christ Star guide you. May you be the Christ Star to others."

Many of the people still had their stars at the worship service on the following Sunday. The stories which were shared were particularly moving. Many people had encountered and been blessed by the Christ Star.

OTHERS OUTSIDE THE GROUP

A youth group in Oregon wanted to reach out and draw in other youth who were outside the church. The worship design team felt that the best place to urge their members to reach out was the commissioning.

When it came to this part of the service, the teenager who was leading the worship showed the participants a picture of Jesus. (It was a puzzle which had been borrowed from the children's education department of the church.) The pieces were large. On the back of each piece, the team had written the name and phone number of a person who was not coming to youth group.

The leader invited each person to choose a puzzle piece and look on the back. They then shared the blessings which would come to the youth group members if the person became a part of their fellowship. Several worshipers reflected that *they* would be blessed by these new people. (This act of blessing was actually a dry run on how the students could talk to the people.)

As an act of commissioning, each member was charged to contact the person represented by the puzzle piece during the next week. The members were to enable that person to feel the love of Christ in such a way that they would feel comfortable coming to this fellowship. They would give the puzzle piece to the person after the invitation.

At the next worship service, the pieces were collected and the picture of Jesus was assembled. Many new guests were present.

EASTER PEOPLE

During the Palm Sunday (week before Easter) morning class, a youth group in New Mexico worshiped with the account of the Resurrection found in John 20:1-18. The portions of the story actually became their order of worship. For instance, the first verse was the call to worship. The youth group members played the roles of the characters in the story. The commissioning act was verse 17 ("... go to my brethren ..."). Each worshiper was given a small stone. The students were instructed to carry this Resurrection stone during the next week and tell others about the joy of the coming Easter event.

At the next session, the youth group members shared the response they had to their attempt to bring the news of Jesus to others.

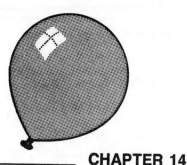

CHAPTER 14

The Table of Love

The table or the shared meal plays an important role in the history of the human community: Food is necessary to life. The gathering of people for nurture has always carried special significance. Whether people partook of food by squatting near a campfire or by sitting at the king's table, the sharing of the meal was and still is the foundation of "kinship."

In the Old Testament, the hospitality of sharing bread has a special meaning. When one was invited to be a guest at the table, he or she became part of the "kinship" or "life spirit" of the tribe. The host had the responsibility for the total well-being of the guest. If the stranger was murdered, the host was charged with the responsibility to avenge such an outrage.

In the New Testament, Jesus' ministry is put into focus through table experiences. His fellowship with tax collectors and sinners made him a marked man in the eyes of the religious authorities of the time. The people knew Jesus had chosen to be "kin" with those who were rejected.

In the Last Supper, Jesus demonstrates the nature of servanthood, the reality of forgiveness and the promise of his return. The Emmaus road experience sharpens our understanding of the role played by table celebrations in Jesus' name. The disciples bumped into a stranger who taught them about the scripture in such a way that they found their hearts racing. When the disciples invited the stranger to eat with them at the table, the Holy Spirit enabled the disciples to see that it was Christ who was present. The hospitality of their act triggered the revelation.

Many themes emerge around the Messianic feast. Each Christian tradition seems to treat this complex subject differently. Some heritages preserve the Eucharistic act as a miracle in which the elements of blood and wine actually become the body and blood of Christ. These churches have well-established traditions on how this celebration should be performed; for example, only certain people can administer the elements.

Other Christian traditions believe that the Lord's Supper is a memorial celebration. They celebrate it often or very infrequently. In these traditions, any believer can serve the bread and wine for the supper. Other Christian traditions fall inbetween these two examples.

This chapter focuses on the creative celebration of the Lord's Supper. If your tradition will not allow for alternate ways to celebrate the Lord's Supper, then use these ideas as "love feasts." This informal gathering was the practice of the early church when it offered thanks to God for every meal. Most traditions permit the love feast as an informal celebration, so please understand the difficulty of discussing this part of worship when so many views are represented by our readers. Feel free to shape the ideas of this chapter within the perimeters of your tradition.

For the sake of clarity, let me share my view of the Lord's Supper. I feel that the Holy Spirit is operative in the Lord's Supper; it is more than a memory event for me. I believe that Christ is present in the sacrament of communion and that the miracle of his presence does not stay in my memory. Christ meets me in this feast.

So much of my Christian experience has unfolded at the table of the Lord. One of the miracles of the feast is that I sit with the communion of saints. Spiritual kin from all ages gather through the Holy Spirit in the Eucharist. I am not alone in my pain, confusion, sin and joy. My roots reveal themselves as I commune with brothers and sisters from the past, present and future. Every time of spiritual renewal has been accompanied by frequent celebration of communion.

I see in the table a rich blending of Christ's message to

our time. As I eat with Christ and my neighbors, I am conscious of the others who cannot feast. The hungry, lost, imprisoned, and abused are most readily present with me as I partake of the bread and wine. The sense of cleansing, renewing and commissioning pours over me.

There is also mystery and power in this act of worship. I mourn for the young who have not experienced this kind of celebration. It is unfortunate if some children in worship pick up the attitude of many of their parents, an attitude of boredom. The world simply has no substitute for the reality of the table which Christ gives us. While these thoughts may or may not be compatible with your communion tradition, don't deny your youth the opportunity to make the love feast a part of their life together.

I don't advocate a loose and off-handed approach to a love feast such as serving pop and chips. Although a love feast is an informal gathering, there also should be a sense of reverence. The Holy Spirit is present whenever God's people gather around the Word. To do anything in remembrance of him is to act in the presence of Christ.

This chapter includes several ideas developed by people around the country concerning the love feast of the Lord. Let these authentic experiences awaken your approach to the feast aspect of your youth worship.

A FEAST OF FOOLS

A youth group in Washington was holding a special Mardi Gras celebration (Shrove Tuesday—the last day before Lent). One of the members called the community to worship with an outstanding trumpet solo. The youth marched in a parade through the church to the music of "When the Saints Go Marching In," then danced in circles and squares.

When it came to the concluding love feast, the group focused on being fools in the eyes of the world (1 Corinthians 3:18). The worship leader passed around a colorful clown wig. Each person was asked to share an experience in which he or she was embarrassed for doing something foolish. The leader read the passage, and the group talked about the singing, dancing and playing which they had just enjoyed. They then feasted on bread and cheese.

THE WATERMELON LOVE FEAST

The youth fellowship was extremely involved in the workcamp; the North Carolina summer sun was blazing. The city young people were deeply touched by the rural poverty. The project forced them to work on repairing the nearly flat church roof. The heat had built to a point where they could no longer work.

The team gathered in the shade of a huge tree with some of the people who worshiped at the church. The teenager in charge of worship read the account of the Last Supper in Matthew 26:17-29.

There was a watermelon sitting in the middle of this circle of tired and thirsty teenagers. The leader passed it around and asked each person to share how the watermelon helped him or her understand the passage.

It was amazing how the students found a relationship between the watermelon and the passage. For example, one native of the area talked about how the watermelon had become the symbol of poor people.

After praying in a circle, the worship leader took a knife, cut the melon and gave the worshipers pieces of it.

THE SASSAFRAS FEAST

One adult leader for a youth group in Illinois enjoys the special warmth which table events bring to the fellowship of the group. One weekend the group members had a great time sliding on the snow at a nearby hill on pieces of plastic. After coming in from the cold, the group participated in a worship experience. The leader set a rough sassafras root in the center of the worship circle.

He read Isaiah 53 which talks about the suffering servant who is like a root out of dry ground. Bill passed the root around the group and asked each person to share how the rough plant related to the person being described in the passage. Many comments were offered about its ugliness.

Bill passed the root around again and asked the group to share how certain ugliness can be beautiful. The leader then showed the group members a root which he had cleaned. This time he invited them to smell it while passing it around. Bill read the passage again and poured out cups of hot sassafras tea which he had brewed before the worship service. He asked the group to describe the taste and feeling of the warm tea. Bill invited them to relate this feeling with the role of the servant in Isaiah 53.

CLEANING UP FOR THE MEAL

A Pennsylvania youth group was participating in a summer youth camp. The worship team was strongly affected by the foot washing of early New Testament times (John 13:1-20). They wanted to refer to this practice for their love feast. It was important that their hands were clean, symbolically and realistically, because the students would be taking turns feeding each other.

The team decided to modify the act to fit their situation. The love feast took place during the time of the closing meal. Three teenagers were at each door of the dining room. One had a bar of soap and pan of water; the second held a towel; the third had a nice-smelling lotion.

Each person was invited to offer his or her hands for washing. The youth were cleansed in a very caring manner. Next, the teenagers were passed on to the person with the towel for drying. After that, the third person gently rubbed the lotion onto the dried hands.

This washing experience took place without conversation. Before the act began, the worshiping community did a simple chant. Then they fed each other the meal.

SHALOM STONES

A youth group from Washington planned a special communion service for New Year's Eve. The presence of Jesus was the major theme. The planning team discovered that the Hebrew term for peace was complex; however, three things emerged:

1. It is always a corporate gift, something to experience in community.

2. It is very political in nature and has to do with a fully integrated and just society.

3. It is a very concrete and everyday sort of thing, not a pie-in-the-sky, out-there-somewhere concept.

At the conclusion of the communion service, the youth passed out rocks. This act was reminiscent of the Hebrew custom of building altars out of "shalom stones" (stones that were solid and well-formed). The stones symbolized what "shalom" meant to the Hebrews.

These rocks were passed to each person in the youth group. These stones were a concrete symbol the youth could take from the service to remind them of their role as peacemakers.

After each person had a rock in his or her hand, the members all joined in a silent prayer for peace. The communion service concluded with the singing of "They Will Know We Are Christians by Our Love."

THE FAMILY CHALICE

Some Wisconsin churches have a special confirmation program; they work with the entire family as a young person prepares for the act of publicly confessing his or her faith. The parents must participate in the six-month experience even if they have accompanied other children through the same program.

One of the high points of the experience is the concluding communion service when the teenagers confess their faith in Jesus Christ. During one session, the teenagers and their parents worked with a church member who was a potter. The potter helped every family make its own chalice. The families designed their own "faith" coat of arms to decorate the communion cup. The chalices were fired, then used by each family during the final communion service The practice was meaningful for all involved.

THE ANTIDOTE AGAINST DEATH

As the planning team was organizing its part in the communion service, the youth pastor shared a teaching in the Apostolic Fathers (Ignatius' Letter to the Ephesians, section 20). The person who lived after the first generation Christians compared the Lord's Supper to a "medicine of immortality" and an "antidote against death." This unique information sparked an idea for the planning team. The members asked an adult sponsor (who was also a nurse) to collect different kinds of extremely small pill bottles.

During the service, a teenager read the passage from

Ignatius. She then passed around a picture of Martin Luther King. She asked the worshipers to share the way by which this understanding of the Lord's Supper (medicine of immortality) was confirmed or challenged by Dr. King's death.

During the Lord's Supper, the wine was distributed in the pill containers.

A FEAST OF FORGIVENESS

Joe was stunned by the strong collusion of feelings in the youth group; a number of smaller groups had formed which tended to split the unity that needs to be part of a faith community.

Joe decided to draw upon the sense of forgiveness and reconciliation which is at the heart of the communion ex- perience. At the end of an overnight retreat, Joe spoke about these aspects of the Lord's Supper. He asked the students to close their eyes and imagine five people in the group with whom they were suffering relationship problems.

After a few minutes, Joe asked each person to go to the altar and choose five flowers from the arrangement prepared before the service. Then Joe invited the students to give the blossoms to the five people in the room.

It was striking how this simple act of reconciliation changed those in the room. There were many hugs and tears as the students came together; the resulting communion service was powerful.

THE MIRACLE OF THE WATER

The new youth minister had just come to the church. The youth had planned a retreat; and Bill found himself a stranger in the midst of these people.

The youth asked Bill to conduct the communion service. He decided to combine this situation with the story of the wedding at Cana.

When the service began, the youth leader read the story (John 2:1-11). He served the students bread and small communion glasses containing water. Bill told the students that Jesus began his ministry by turning water into wine. It was Bill's prayer that as the teenagers took the water, the Holy Spirit would bless the water so that it would become wine in them. He prayed that their ministry together would also be blessed as a miracle. This was one communion service that the students would never forget.

THE LIVING WINE

The teenagers were in charge of a worship service at the end of a daylong conference. They came up with a creative option for communion and chose John 15:1-11 as the theme. The group knew that the teenagers attending the conference would not be together this way again.

They obtained loaves of fresh bread and bunches of grapes. When the time came to drink from the cup, the teenagers passed around the grapes. Each person was invited to celebrate the love feast by taking a grape. The biblical images concerning the grapes evoked strong feelings in the students as they ate them.

The students then joined hands and talked about being a part of the living vine. This bond would last throughout eternity since Christ is the living branch of life.

THE COMMUNION OF SAINTS

While the worship team of young people was planning for the next youth worship service, someone mentioned that a member of the youth fellowship was facing the divorce of her parents. The team members realized that several people in the youth group were in the same situation. Difficult questions arose such as, "How do the youth choose the parent with whom to live?" One boy asked how many people had grandparents in the area; only one hand went up.

The youth adviser said the church provides a sense of family. We belong to a kinship which goes back 4,000 years. People started adding names of people, both living and dead, who are a part of this chain. From this diversified conversation came the idea to focus on the "kinship chain" for communion or a love feast. Jesus said, "As often as you eat and drink, do this in remembrance of me."

The team members searched everywhere for photos and drawings of spiritual kin such as Abraham, Sarah, Moses, Isaiah, Mary, Paul, church fathers and mothers, historical figures and contemporary Christians. They gathered quotes from each of these people's history. The team gathered enough pictures for each person in the class, also utilizing the same number of candles.

When the entire youth group came to the room for worship, they were given the pictures and quotes. They were asked to spend a couple minutes studying this person who was a spiritual relative.

The lights were turned down and a candle was lighted to represent Jesus as the "light of the world." A box of matches was passed around the circle. Each person showed his or her picture and shared the quote. Then the person was invited to light a candle for the biblical person and share how he or she provided something which helped the student become part of the faith family.

These candles were placed in small lumps of modeling clay. The youth then sang a special hymn of the church and shared bread and cheese; fruit juice also was served. The worship leader asked each person to offer a toast for a member of the spiritual family who most deeply touched his or her life.

THE BREAD OF LIFE

Bread and baked goods seem to play a consistent role in the ways Christians celebrate the love feast. The bread may be made with a number of different grains, leavened or unleavened, and in just about every shape.

Utilize the baking skills of your young people or others in the congregation. Some groups have intentionally chosen breads from different cultures for love feasts celebrating the transcultural dimension of the Christian faith. Other people have built the baking of bread right into the worship service. A small youth group can meet in the kitchen of the church and can spend some time reflecting on the grain from which the flour comes. How does its destruction help us learn something about Jesus?

Youth group members can make individual loaves or shape the communion bread into the form of fish. This emphasizes the biblical theme of the loaves and fish; it is amazing how well these shapes turn out.

Such a model can then lead to a discussion of the hungry people who will not be at the table. This is particularly powerful when the worshipers are hungry themselves and can smell the baking bread. The final celebration of the love feast comes with the breaking of the bread and the drinking of the juice. Imagine making grape juice from fresh grapes *and* baking bread!

One youth group in the Pittsburgh area bakes bread each Saturday to raise money for the hunger program and workcamps. This activity combines Christian worship and service.

A Michigan youth group makes biscuits for their love feast. They have found that each person can create his or her own special mix. Some add orange juice and other ingredients which bring something special to the bread. Then they share the loaves with each other.

REFRESHING REFRESHMENTS

Every youth group tends to share refreshments whenever it meets. This time has been an established part of youth ministry. Yet, there is a danger that we take such times of eating too casually. The refreshment time can be the perfect time for a love feast.

A youth group in Pennsylvania demonstrates this approach. Instead of taking a break from the gathering, the group ties its eating in with the whole evening's program. For example, one evening the members were asked to choose a potato and prepare it for baking. These were then wrapped in aluminum foil and thrown into the fireplace or baked in the oven.

At refreshment time, the youth gathered to retrieve their potatoes. While the potatoes were cooling, the youth read Matthew 27:45-50 and shared how the potatoes told them about the account of Jesus' suffering.

The students then prepared the potatoes by adding butter, bacon bits, cheese and other items. They shared a prayer of thanksgiving for this food and ate. This model is simple as well as meaningful and healthful.

The love feast, as celebrated in relationship to refreshments, can easily be adapted to just about every setting and food. One of the unfortunate aspects of the overindulging parts of the world is that those who can eat in abundance do not eat with joy and celebration.

How do we help young people to taste the wonder of food with thanksgiving? One way is to approach the eating time as a worshipful act. Handle the food as if it is of immense value. If God gives us this daily bread, it is worthy and must be treated with care and honor. Eat slowly, savor each bite and give thanks to God for the blessing of food.

THE TABLE EXERCISE

The table exercise is a worship attitude which enables a young person to consider all eating occasions in a Christian perspective. These moments are intentional opportunities to acknowledge Christ as the Lord of life and to acknowledge the importance of the kinship of faith. These opportunities are most often utilized in family settings.

The table exercise includes the following five attributes: a Bible verse, a table item or food, reflection on the verse, eating the food and giving thanks.

Here are five examples which might be used when the group is eating together on a field trip or at a fast-food place.

1. Read James 3:17-18 aloud. Pass a salt shaker around the table. Shake a few grains into each person's hand. Ask diners to share how this ancient substance symbolizes wisdom and righteousness today. For example, "Just as wisdom is pure, so is this salt—white and pure." Close with a circle prayer. Ask each person to include the word "wisdom" in his or her prayer.

2. Read 1 Kings 4:22-25 aloud. Pick up one of the food dishes (grain, vegetable or hamburger) and pass it around the table. Have each person share how the item could be used to bring peace between themselves and another nation. For example, "We could supply food to needy nations and help them fully utilize their resources." Focus the prayer circle on the hungry.

3. Read Matthew 25:31-46 aloud. Place a dish or item of food before each person. Have the diners describe the

food as if it were being sold in an ad. For example, "The world's most crispy french fries." Read a story about a hungry person which you have clipped from a newspaper. Focus the prayer circle on the starving people of the world. Close with each person tasting a small portion of food and giving thanks.

4. Read Jeremiah 29:11 aloud. Ask each person to pick up a fork and share how it symbolizes his or her life story and God's plan. For example, "Just as this fork helps me to nourish my body, God helps me to nourish my faith and life through his caring, the Word and his Son." Close with a prayer circle of thanksgiving for a hopeful future.

5. Psalm 33:16-22 aloud. Pass a small mirror around the table. Ask students to share their thoughts if this reflection was the only thing God saw about their lives. What shield does God provide? Focus the prayer circle on the protection of faith which God gives to each person.

THE VIDEO FEAST

A youth group in a remote area in Tennessee had the responsibility of producing the church's access cable channel show.

One Sunday they suggested that the pastor conduct a service for those at home, using only one camera. They played upon the media's greatest attribute: intimacy. The pastor asked the people living in the hills to take bread and juice or wine and celebrate communion along with him on television.

A lady wrote to the church and thanked the young people and the pastor for making this table available to her. She said that she and her husband took bread and wine in their home as the service was being telecast. Her husband had died very recently. She expressed her appreciation to the church for providing this last opportunity of taking the sacrament together.

Television cannot take the place of the personal experience of being in the same room with brothers and sisters; however, this ministry enables people who are unable to attend worship to be touched by the Lord's Supper in a special way.

CHAPTER 15

Baptism

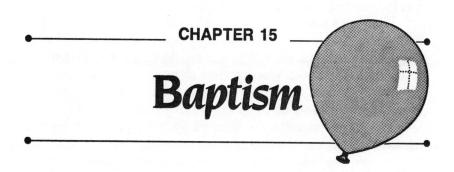

The mystery and power of water underscores the very formation of creation. The Spirit of God moved across the face of the waters as the world was created. Indeed the human floats in water on the journey to birth. Water sustains us. We go a long time without eating, but we must have liquid to keep the human body functioning.

Water also washes, cleanses and heals. Ancient peoples found special places in their culture for ritual washing. Spiritual cleansing is not far behind in the history of society and religion.

John the Baptist came with a baptism of repentance for those who confessed their faith. Jesus himself submitted to the baptism of John. The followers of Jesus were sent out to baptize in the name of Jesus.

To whom is this circle of cleansing directed? Scholars have struggled over the nature of this important Christian sacrament. Some have found evidence for only the believer's baptism undertaken by those who make a confession of faith. This interpretation focuses on the teenager and the adult.

Other scholars have seen a tradition of having infants baptized. This latter view assumes that in the name of the Trinity, the act of baptism cleanses anyone. But the power rests in the act of God, not on the response of the believer. This viewpoint is usually accompanied by the conviction that baptism is necessary for eternal life. In an emergency, any Christian can baptize those close to death. Your church has made decisions about this question of baptism.

There is also the question concerning the mode of baptism. Christians use immersion, pouring and sprinkling. Again, your church has its tradition.

Like the Lord's Supper, baptism is viewed differently by various traditions. Like so many biblical acts of salvation there are a number of meanings to baptism: cleansing, death of old self and resurrection of new creation, commissioning and membership in the community of faith. Although this portion of worship is not in the hands of teenagers, they are deeply affected by this special moment in their lives.

In this chapter, I will share 10 interesting creative acts which others have developed to celebrate baptism. Some of these ideas show how youth assist in the worship of God as others are baptized. Please work through these clues as you consider how baptism touches the lives of your youth. You will have to filter these ideas through your tradition and practice of baptism. Please don't react quickly because an idea comes from a different perspective from your heritage. Baptism is so important that each true celebration of it brings new insight to every believer.

A HOST OF FLOWERS

The youth adviser, Lou, had worked hard to develop ways by which his youth could minister to others in the church. (Infant baptism was celebrated in their tradition.)

When Lou was teaching the youth about their understanding of baptism, it became clear that the congregation was actually a partner in the act involving the child. The parents and the infant needed the support of other believers. How could the youth participate in this part of the faith development of the youngest among them?

The group members struggled with this question. They focused on how they could contribute something to the worship service which would affirm that the child was being welcomed into the community of faith. One of the teenagers was skilled in sewing. With the help of the other members, she created a large banner with the words, "Bring the children to me."

The youth group started a tradition by which each

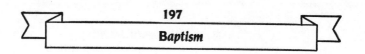

family bringing a child for baptism received a small cloth flower. The child's name was sewn into it. The flower was added to the banner at the time of baptism. The banner soon had clusters of flowers as children were baptized. It is displayed during the Sundays when baptisms are celebrated.

THE RIVER JORDAN

One Illinois church practiced "believer" baptism. Adults were regularly immersed in the water of the baptistry. Unfortunately, the church was built in such a way that it appeared quite gloomy for these moments of joy and thanksgiving.

The youth group members were talking about their baptism experiences when the problem of the setting came up. The youth adviser asked them how they could improve the situation. They all went into the sanctuary and looked at the baptistry.

One teenager was a photographer. He suggested that they could show a slide on the back wall if the service was at night. The others liked the idea. They found a number of slides in the Christian education department. The group members couldn't believe it when they found a slide of the river Jordan! It had been taken in the middle of the river so it looked as if the viewer was actually in the Jordan.

One teenager placed the slide projector so that it could not be seen from where the worshipers were sitting. (However, by showing the slide on the wall behind the baptistry, it looked exactly as if the person was being baptized in the Jordan.) The youth group called the pastor; he came over to this meeting. The pastor was very pleased by the dramatic setting created by this simple slide.

The church now used the slide for all evening baptisms. This is another example of youth ministering to the whole church.

BRING THE CHILDREN

Peter was getting baptized as a teenager. This was unusual in his church because most people experienced this sacrament as infants. The pastor worked with him concerning the meaning of this event.

At first Peter felt a bit embarrassed about this public act. The minister explained that his decision was a moment which would bless everyone at the church service. Whenever baptism takes place, every worshiper experiences the Gospel in an enacted form.

As they talked, the pastor suggested that he and Peter do something special so that Peter could intentionally contribute something important to the whole church. They focused on the children who were present. How could they involve them in Peter's confession of faith and baptism?

Peter agreed to be the only person to be baptized or welcomed into membership. The pastor was a very sensitive person and decided to spend the time necessary in the service to make the event memorable.

When the time came for the baptism, the pastor invited the children to come to the front of the church. Peter and the minister stood at the baptismal font. They took the bowl of water and asked the children to put their fingers in it. The pastor and Peter talked with the youngsters about the role water played in their lives.

The pastor told the children that Peter was going to be baptized. He asked them if they knew what that meant. Peter was then encouraged to share why he had decided to be baptized. He told the children about Jesus and how Jesus had touched his life. It was a simple but moving testimony. As Peter tried to explain things to the children, the witness seemed to grow in authenticity and power. There were tears in the eyes of many adults.

The children remained with the pastor and Peter as they moved to the ceremony of baptism. The young ones were utterly engrossed by being a part of this experience. Peter knelt as the minister and assisting adults baptized him with sprinkling.

The pastor encouraged the children to place their hands on Peter as he was blessed. This teenager's baptism became a means of grace for the young and old at worship. Peter's parents claim that they could see a difference in Peter's life since he was baptized.

INTO MATURITY

In this book, we have noted the importance of celebration passage rites. Baptism may be the most important rite of maturity facing the young person in his or her teenage years.

One family was deeply impressed by the maturation rites of Jewish families. They designed their own way of celebrating the teenager baptism passage point for their family. When each of their children reached the age when the church encouraged them to be baptized, they planned a special family celebration.

The mother interviewed the teenager about his or her heroes and heroines such as rock stars, sports figures, politicians, actors and actresses, etc. The teenager also chose his or her favorite menu. The parents then developed their own table liturgy for the big passage celebration.

After each youth had been baptized in church, the family gathered at home for the special dinner. Candles were lighted and the worship service of thanksgiving for the teenager was offered. The parents then presented a special scrapbook to the young person. The mother had written to the teenager's heroes and heroines and the book contained their answers. She told these rock stars, sports figures, and politicians that the teenager was celebrating his or her baptism and that the hero (heroine) was an important model. The mother never had a famous person not write back; many of the letters were quite extensive.

This model is an excellent example of how the baptized teenager can be surrounded by love and affirmation. Encourage such practices among the parents of your youth.

Many adult youth leaders have attempted to take the role of the parents. This attempt is senseless because youth leaders only have the young people for a short time. We as youth leaders need to equip parents to do the job they often wish they could do, but lack the ability or confidence. We are called to enable others to do ministry.

ONE ON ONE

Baptism is always the most meaningful when it draws upon the reservoir of spiritual preparation. Many churches have recognized this when it comes to teenagers.

A church in Arkansas has a carefully developed program of preparation for believer baptism. Six months before the teenagers plan to confess their faith and accept baptism, they each are assigned an adult in an apprentice or mentor relationship. Ken, the pastor, works with the baptism mentors so that this sponsorship can nurture a genuine Christian kinship.

The pairs meet weekly as a total group with the pastor. They focus on Christian theology, discipleship and community building as teams. Many of the adults will take the teenagers to their work. This especially arises when a young person is seeking a vocational choice.

The adults regularly report that they receive a great deal from their relationship with these young Christians. The pairing of teenagers with old members of the congregation also has been particularly successful. Many young people do not have grandparents in the area where they live. There is something very special about how baptism links the connection between generations of faith. The opportunity of the young and old exploring their faith together provides an important preparation for baptism.

The worship service in which the baptism takes place involves these mentors. Ken does not believe in having serial baptisms. Each service, he only focuses on one young person and his or her mentor. This pastor believes that each time a person confesses his or her faith and receives baptism, the Gospel is experienced by everyone present. Such a moment in salvation history is too important to be experienced in the form of mass production.

At the service, the mentor presents the young person for baptism. These words of testimony and affirmation on behalf of the young person are a very important part of the baptismal event. The experience often rings of the heavenly voice in the baptism of Jesus and says, loud and clear, that the young person is beloved of the Lord and the faith community. There are not many places in our society where the young are affirmed as individuals. If you achieve according to the systems of the culture (sports, academics, behavior patterns, etc.), the rewards are there. However, teenagers are not loved unconditionally except by Christ.

After the teenager has confessed his or her faith and received baptism, the mentor presents a symbol to remind the young person that Christ will always be with him or her. These symbols have ranged from rings to crosses. Those who have been through this program bear witness to the extreme amount of power in this baptism event.

WHAT CHILD IS THIS

As we have noted, infant baptism (or dedication) implies that both the parents and the congregation are participants in the convenant. They must be the ones who will aid the child in growing as a disciple of Christ. Yet, this is not often celebrated in worship. Most congregations have the worshipers agree to a statement about such support, but worship demands more than this.

At a church in Ohio, two youth advisers were particularly loved by the teenagers and other members. The advisers had wanted children for a long time. Finally, they were to become parents and everyone was delighted. The youth group felt very much a part of this happy couple's excitement. The teenagers were thrilled when Amy was born.

The youth group members asked the pastor how they could play a role in the baptism of the new child. The couple was happy that they wanted to be part of the service. This would reflect the family of faith into which the baby girl would live, grow and learn about the Lord.

The service of baptism was designed so that the youth and the young children were part of it. The youth worked for several months on a most unusual gift: a baby-blanket quilt. Several older women helped them as they created a number of amazingly complex cloth scenes from the life of the youth group which had been shared with this loving couple.

For the baptism, the couple was seated in two chairs in the center of the worship area. After the baby was baptized, the youth gathered around the seated family, placed their hands on them, saying prayers of thanksgiving and intercession. Each teenager contributed a sentence or more to the group prayer, then the quilt was wrapped around the child.

The pastor concluded the service by sprinkling water on the teenagers and on the congregation as he walked down the aisle. He was reminding them that they were all baptized into the kinship of Christ.

CLEANSING WATER

Pilate turned to water in an attempt to wash his hands of responsibility for the fate of Jesus. Lady Macbeth was driven by her madness to wash away her bloody hands. There are many teenagers who feel the sting of sin's uncleanliness. Most churches have not developed a means by which the regeneration and cleansing of baptism is experienced anew daily. Our baptism is an ongoing process which never ends; Christ is always washing away our sins.

One youth group in Iowa drew upon this reality by utilizing water as the symbolic reminder of their baptism. The living water of salvation is an important biblical theme. The "birth" day wash is a weekly opportunity to celebrate the baptism of someone in the group. The youth group gathers the dates of each member's baptism. The closest date is celebrated in worship on that particular week. This research often takes a lot of time because those who were baptized as children may not know the date.

When the time in the service comes for this emphasis, the person whose "birth" day is being celebrated is introduced. Then water is used in some way to remember the saving power of this moment in the person's life. One week they chose a biblical passage which used water to teach the cleansing power of God's love (Acts 22:16).

They asked the person to share something about his or her baptism which is remembered by others. This is often a time of laughter. The worship leader affirmed to the person that God's baptism is still changing his or her life. Sometimes, they have the "birth" day person go around and wash the hands of each member as a way of sharing this reminder of God's love in each life.

Each week this portion of the service is a bit different. One week they asked the "birth" day person to share God's gift of new life by using water to make the outline of the cross on each forehead. Each face was then gently patted dry with a towel.

This weekly celebration of baptism became powerful. Don't reject this model because it has not been your experience. The young (and the old) need a regular recital of God's saving moments in their lives. There is no reason why the act of baptism cannot be kept before your people as a great gift of God.

IN THE RIVER

Traditions which celebrate immersion usually utilize a tank or pool in a portion of the church. This baptistry provides a very meaningful setting for baptism; however, there is nothing as moving as an outdoor setting. The whole worshiping congregation is suddenly cast back to the Jordan river. They are actually in the biblical setting. It takes just a bit of spiritual imagination to be with John the Baptist as he baptizes Jesus.

Weather, location and modern conditions make it difficult for these kinds of settings to be practical for all baptisms. Yet, a camp or some other location can be used to give youth a special experience. There must be extra precaution when undertaking baptism in natural settings.

Even if a young person is not being baptized at this outdoor event, remember there is a special proclamation made to every person present when another accepts Christ.

UNTO DEATH

There are Christian traditions which believe that every person needs baptism in order to live eternally with God. They have worked out ways by which the unbaptized also win this victory. However, it becomes imperative that any Christian baptize another who is close to death and has not been baptized. This may or may not be your tradition. Yet, the urgency of this sign of God's love is important for every Christian to understand. Youth particularly need to experience the life and death aspect of God's saving signs.

Invite a nurse or doctor to your worship service. These professionals are often called upon to baptize people close to death. A few inquiries will easily find such a person.

I remember when I was serving as a full-time chaplain in a children's hospital which dealt with many hopeless cases. One evening the nurse told me that a couple wanted to talk with me. I had been calling on their young son for the past three weeks. They said that they were worried and wanted their son baptized. I was a young seminarian and my tradition rooted baptism in the congregational setting. In fact, I was officially permitted to baptize anyone. We talked about it—the couple also came from the same tradition. It was agreed that they would wait to baptize their son until they returned to their home church.

It was 2 a.m. when the call came from the nurse. The couple wanted to see me. When I arrived at the hospital, I found that the little boy's medical situation had worsened. It was likely that he would die in the next few hours. The couple, overwhelmed with grief, wanted to be assured of God's love. I realized that there was only one way that they could experience this assurance.

When I baptized the child a few minutes later, a peace came over the parents. When their son died a few hours later, they felt secure in the knowledge that he was with the Lord.

It is this kind of story which your young people need to hear in terms of the importance baptism plays in people's lives. Such a visitor could offer the sermon or perhaps fit into the baptism segment as suggested in the previous model.

THE BAPTISM OF THE SAINTS

Another way to lift up the memory of baptism as part of your youth worship services is to seek the stories of other Christians concerning baptism. This can be done quite easily. Choose a person each week to be in charge of this portion of the worship service; loan him or her an

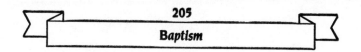

audio cassette recorder. Have this person seek an older Christian and interview him or her about his or her baptism.

This process will accomplish two important things: The older person will be delighted by this affirmation of interest in his or her faith experience and the youth will meet some of the most special people they will ever encounter.

After the interview, carefully select segments from the tape so that the group will not be bored. Most people can only listen for a short time span. When you come to the baptism section of the service, play the tape. Invite the students to share how this particular story relates to their own baptism or something which the Bible tells us about baptism.

Conclude with a prayer circle focusing on this saint in Christ.

CHAPTER 16

Fifteen Complete Worship Services

We love to get what we need in nice packages. Yet, it is often best to put the pieces together ourselves. The goal of this book is to encourage you to create your own worship services with youth.

In this chapter, I will share 15 complete worship services that are designed for youth Sundays, evening services, Bible studies, retreats, workcamps, etc. I suggest that you outline these ideas according to the storyboard format shared in Chapter 1. The storyboard helps you to organize the service and make sure all details are covered.

Up to this point in the book, I have given you many bits and pieces. Authentic worship of God flows and seems to come from one single source. In fact, when we are in midst of the worship experience, we may not even be aware of the individual sections. Yet, it is important that we treasure each part of the worship as we design the whole piece.

Before we piece together the different parts of a worship service, it is important to face questions about the participants. When are the people gathering for your service? Is the context for worship a retreat? evening service? Sunday morning class? What is it that God has to say to us at this moment?

These are difficult questions which can never be answered completely. We simply don't know our people and God well enough to speak for them. Yet, these concerns are vital to the creation of a meaningful worship service.

Most worship events need to contain the basic ingredients which have been included in this book. Yet, the flow of the worship can be organized into just about any sequence which fits the answers to the questions raised above. For instance, a service for a day of grief could begin with prayers of intercession or supplication. At a happier time, thanksgiving prayer acts could be an appropriate approach to God.

The same sort of flexibility is fitting for the rest of the service. I have seen youth groups design powerful celebrations which literally present the worship event in the opposite order of the usual service (benediction first, etc.). In seminary we used to refer to the ACTS when we talked about prayers for worship. The letters reminded us of the following: Adoration; Confession and pardon; Thanksgiving; and Supplication (intercession and petition). It is easy to put them in any order: SACT, CATS, TACS or TCAS.

Many youth services are very informal. People tend to sing a couple songs, pray, read some scripture and then hear some preaching. While these kinds of experiences can be meaningful, I urge you to consider all of the attributes of worship as you plan. While our needs are important in worship, we are still meeting the Lord of all creation and we are confronted with an agenda more complete than our own.

It is also important to know how much time you have for the worship service. We either have too little time or too much time for worship. The kinds of worship services in this book tend to draw youth into the experience. This means that the worship services take more time than the traditional service which focuses on printed words and follows the worship leader. Allow one to two hours for each worship, depending on the number of participants.

You may decide that the creative worships in this chapter will be too disorienting for those who have been raised on the usual Sunday morning form of worship. We must remember that the worship of God is not a show or entertainment, but it can be exciting and entertaining. Do not choose change for the sake of innovation; choose change as a means of presenting God's message in new wineskins.

It helps to maintain emotional continuity when you change. People (young people as well as older adults) tend to be very conservative about their basic emotional moorings. They do not want their worlds turned upside down in areas where they look for security. The young can give up an old worship approach only when they have a new mode which they can fully and freely embrace.

When you create your own worship services, you may be shocked to get a negative reaction from your young people. You may be a nervous wreck and they may not show their excited affirmation because of your changing worship. This is to be expected.

Your introductory approach can be a slow one. For example, change only one piece of the usual service. Or just lead the teenagers through one worship segment in one of the other settings in which you work (class, workcamp, etc.). The young can give their honest affirmation only on what they have experienced. Once they have felt the power of creative worship, they then can become very excited about it.

ENCORE APPEARANCE

I have chosen some typical settings for the following services. You may note that some of these ideas have been your favorite worship techniques for years. In fact, you will notice that ideas shared in this book will be used in different ways for different purposes. Flexibility is one of the important ingredients to the creative process.

The way you shape a worship idea to your place and your people will make even the oldest idea very special. Worship is one area of theology where one need not worry about being trendy. The old and new mix and develop together beautifully. The oldest worship practice may be the very best for those who have never experienced it.

TRUST YOUR HERITAGE

Try not to duplicate the following services; feel free to

modify, adjust, add, subtract, and change these outlines to fit your tradition and special needs. I am fully aware that you have a very special liturgical heritage which will cast a unique light on everything in this book. Follow these important insights as you view our creative starting points.

Your young people often do not know many of the historical traditions upon which their faith is celebrated. One of the best ways to enrich your liturgical outlook is to review the liturgical history of your faith heritage.

GOODBYE, LONE RANGER

Be sure that your teenagers work with you on creating your order of worship. Adults working with youth have to struggle with the "caretaking" approach to youth work. We must enable youth to worship, study, serve and have fellowship.

The "Lone Ranger" style of designing creative worship will soon fail. One person can't be the source of endless ideas if he or she works alone. After two or three times of solo planning, you will run out of energy and ideas. Creative worship comes out of the community to serve the community of faith. We are much more complete in the context of creative brothers and sisters.

YOUTH SUNDAY

Many churches have a special Sunday for youth to take over the leadership of morning worship. Such moments can be very exciting because of the novelty, yet very disappointing because of the resistance.

I suggest that the traditional order of worship be retained. Youth groups who totally change the service are being unfair to the adults who expect continuity in this important part of their faith experience. Again, worship is not an entertainment piece. The youth have the awing responsibility of leading the congregation in their relationship with God. Yet, the perspective of youth is unique and important.

Involve the whole youth group in the planning and implementation of this service. It is tempting to select three or four of the best readers and have them lead the celebration. However, the contribution of the youth is their active presence.

Psalms are the best source of scripture verses for the call to worship. For instance, choose the first three verses of Psalm 95.

"O come, let us sing to the Lord;
let us make a joyful noise to the rock of our salvation!
Let us come into his presence with thanksgiving;
Let us make a joyful noise to him with songs of praise!
For the Lord is a great God,
and a great King above all gods."

Have one of your members introduce the call to worship by saying, "Let us worship God by seeing and hearing God's invitation to worship." Instead of reading the Psalm in unison, involve the eyes of the worshipers by having several members of the youth fellowship "sign" the words as they are read slowly by one of your members. Ask a member of the congregation or someone in the community to help with this sign language. The use of the hands to communicate these words of hope and promise will be very moving.

Develop a musical version of the prayer act of invocation. This can be done by working with the choir director. Pick a few lines from one of the Psalms. Encourage your music person to design the singing of the Psalm in such a way that the choir sings one line and the congregation the next.

You could choose two lines which speak about the Holy Spirit. The teenagers who lead this section of the service could use simple mime motions for each word. They can encourage the worshipers to follow them in the movements.

Secure a paper clip to each bulletin and distribute them to the worshipers. Ask a youth group member to read a passage about sin; for example, "If we say we have no sin, we deceive ourselves ..." (1 John 1:8).

Have the leader ask the congregation to take the simple paper clip off the bulletin. The leader will direct the congregation to consider their own sinfulness as they bend and reshape the paper clip. The leader can direct the worshipers to shape the clip in such a way that it expresses their feelings about sin in their lives.

After this time of confession, proceed to the prayer act of pardon. While a song is sung, have the teenagers collect the wire sculptures with the offering plates. The leader then gives the biblical assurance that all sin is forgiven through the person and work of Jesus Christ.

Have the worship leader remind the congregation that we are called to bear one another's burdens. Redistribute the paper clips. Ask each person to carry it during the week and pray for the temptations facing the unknown person whose sin is symbolized in the wire shape.

Ask the teenager leading the prayer act of intercession to take the Sunday paper which has been placed on the altar or communion table and announce that this news symbolizes the needs of the world. Have him or her rip the paper into long strips. The ushers will then distribute these strips of paper to the worshipers.

Have the worship leader invite the congregation to participate in the prayer of intercession. The members can call out a concern which they read in their newspaper strip. If the youth are worried about introducing this new form of prayer, prior to the worship alert a few people about this opportunity for sharing so they will be ready to respond.

Everyone can find something to share. The youngest and oldest worshipers are equal in their sensitivity about the suffering of the world. This model of prayer also provides worshipers with strings of continuity between worship and life when they pick up the newspaper after church. They will come across items which were lifted up to God earlier.

Ask the teenager who is leading the prayer act of petition to ask each person to look at his or her hand carefully. As the worshipers look at their hands, have the leader ask some of the following reflective questions (pausing between each one):

"How do the lines and scars on your hand represent your struggles today?"

"Follow one line with your eyes. Are you coming to a dead end in your choices for what you must decide today?"

"Imagine that the lines on your hand are God lines

Where is God leading you?''

After a few seconds, lead a prayer for the needs of those in the room.

Conclude by asking each person to turn and shake hands with another person. Affirm that by reaching out to the needs of another we are assured that Christ meets us in our struggles.

Invite the congregation to offer prayers of thanksgiving. Ask the members of the youth group to stand where they are and offer a few sentences of thanksgiving for something specific. Others in the congregation can contribute to these prayers. After each contribution, lead the congregation in a vocal response such as "O Lord, we thank you."

Read the Old and New Testament lessons. You could use the lectionary lesson if this is your tradition, or you could use selections such as Joel 2:28-29 and 1 Corinthians 13:1-13.

It is important that the Bible passages are read or presented so that the people can focus on the content of the Gospel. These two readings sparkle with imagination and idealism. They beg to be presented with wineskins of this nature. The Old Testament passage could be presented by reading and liturgical movement. Most churches are not used to dancing in worship; however, God has called people throughout history to use their bodies as well as their minds and voices to glorify him. One disciplined dancer can authentically provide an important dimension to the communication of the Bible message.

If you use the dancer, you will have to read the passage in a different manner. You may have to utilize the technique of those who write classical choral music. Cantors also use this method of repeating a biblical verse several times with different vocal readings. This can be easily worked out with reader and dancer.

The New Testament lesson calls for congregation involvement. Use the old frontier methods of "lining" the verses to the congregation. This method was developed when there were not enough copies of the Bible for everyone. The leader says a line and the congregation repeats it. Preparation for this style demands that the verses are divided into easy phrases for short-term memory. People cannot remember long lines with only one hearing.

The sermon can be presented as a role play or interactive drama. I am not suggesting scripts and memorized lines. Choose three people from the youth group before the youth Sunday service. Assign each of them a character to play.

1. The lost teenager ("the child" in 1 Corinthians 13). She thinks like a child about life, parents, school, drugs and the future. She is a runaway who is always in trouble. The person playing this role will need to prepare a two- or three-minute first-person monologue introducing herself.

2. The confused parent. The person assigned this role needs to prepare a short introductory monologue. She can't understand the lost teenager. This person will present the argument which condemn all teenagers such as, "They're so moody, up and down all the time. And their energy level wears me out!"

3. A straight peer. A short opening statement is required from this person. This "nice" teenager does everything that the adult desires. He accepts authority and never questions anything. This person is very judgmental of the lost teenager.

Have the youth group sit on the floor of the worship center. Ask the chosen actors to present their character. Then ask the actors to stay in character and discuss with each other their goals in life. They can make up their parts as they go along. They will not agree and be quite judgmental of each other.

Interrupt them after a couple of minutes and reread the passage. Ask the other students to respond to what has been happening on the drama from the perspective of the passage in 1 Corinthians 13. After the students have interpreted the passage in light of this conflict of values, read the passage again. End this section of worship with a prayer.

Call for the offering. When the ushers have gathered for the collection, play a minute or shorter tape of someone who is a recipient of the church's ministry. This will mean that someone from your group will have to go to a retirement home, hospital or some other area of need for the short comments. Take the offering and prayer for those who will use it to service God.

After the last hymn has been sung, ask the congregation to turn around and face the doorway through which they will depart. Prepare a short charge to be concluded in the name of the Trinity. For example:

"As you face the world into which you are called to serve, be prepared to witness.
Bind up the wounds of those who bled;
comfort those who cry;
bear with those older people who don't understand youth;
have compassion on those young people who are impatient and inconsiderate.
Fulfill your ministry in the name of Father, and the Son and the fellowship of the Holy Spirit."

At the proper places, add music which the congregation knows. Have the youth group host the coffee hour after church. Serve baked goodies and juice. Gain feedback from the worshipers by passing out blank slips of paper and pencils to them as they enter the fellowship hall. Ask them to write down any reflections they have concerning the worship experience. Encourage the worshipers not to sign their names.

After the few minutes, have the young people call the group to order. Read the comments. When there is a word of criticism; acknowledge it with comment. Ask the others in the room to respond to what has been said.

WELCOME A NEW MEMBER

This worship service is designed for the Sunday evening service by the members of the group. In this case, the celebration is part of a local fellowship's outreach to new members. The worship takes place at the home of the new person. Members of the group bring food for a light meal. They meet in front of the new member's home.

Build the service around Exodus 12:7-13. This is the account of the household which is protected from the spirit of death. The passover is a blessing upon the home of the faithful.

As the visitors enter the home with food, lead the people in singing a well-known song which fits the theme of hospitality. Ask a teenager to lead the blessing by reading Proverbs 24:3-4 which talks about the home.

Sing another well-known song which reflects on the spirit of fellowship. Read Exodus 12:7-13. At this point have the youth place a red ribbon around the outside doorway.

Eat the meal together. Ask the teenage worship leader to lead a sharing about how God blesses the stranger and a new home. Lead a prayer of thanksgiving for the newest member of the group and his or her family. Do this by having a prayer circle in which each person adds to the prayer.

Ask a young person to line out the following prayer a verse at a time so that everyone can easily repeat it.

"May this household and those who share its space, o Lord, work long and carefully to make this home a place where the wind of the Holy Spirit dwells, a haven of shalom, a house of unaffected joy, a shelter of prayer, a warehouse of the goods of your kingdom's stewards, a haven of hospitality for the stranger and needy, and a hostel of the Lord of life and love. We do this, God, secure in the knowledge that you have been by here and are here now."

Read Acts 2:44-47 and begin the passing of the peace. Most groups hug each other as a way to testify that God is present.

Join hands in a circle and encourage each person to share a word of affirmation in welcoming the new family and teenager to their fellowship. Give the young person a cross or other symbol of being part of their household of faith.

This simple worship by the youth group has a profound impact on the new person. By going out and honoring the newest among them, the youth are establishing the quality of their Christian fellowship.

WORSHIP IN A BIBLE STUDY

The time for worship in a Bible study or Sunday school class is always limited. However, the quick prayer and business-as-usual approach to worship in educational settings is not adequate.

Acts 2:44-47 indicates that the Christian is always expressed most authentically when he or she celebrates four marks of faithfulness: worship, fellowship, education and the sending out to perform miracles. Shouldn't every church activity include all four? Most all of these facets are not present in many contemporary church gatherings.

The best way of balancing time restrictions with the imperative to worship at all times is to wrap the worship right around the study.

Use Genesis 3:1-24 for this combination Bible study and worship. As the students enter the room, play a tape recording of the sounds of nature (birds, etc.).

Ask the students to close their eyes and imagine that God is inviting them into the presence of the Lord (the call to worship). Ask what particular sound is most inviting to them.

Place a bowl of fruit in the center of a circle of chairs. Read the passage. Pick out an apple or orange and pass it around the circle. Ask each student to share what contemporary sins are symbolized by this piece of fruit (confession).

Pass the fruit around the circle again and ask each person to share how God is telling us something about his forgiveness of our sins in this apple (pardon).

Enter into the lesson for the class (sermon) Allow 30 minutes to study and discuss the passage.

Cut the apple into sections with a small knife. Put these fruit chips on a plate and pass them around the group. Invite each person to take one and eat it (love feast).

Form a prayer circle and focus on the needs of those who don't have the feast of the Lord (intercession). Give each person a piece of fruit and commission him or her to feed someone who needs to be released from the burden of sin. Ask the youth to share their experiences at the next class. For a more complete look at this style of study and worship, look at **Dennis Benson's Creative Bible Studies** (studies on every passage in the four Gospels and Acts) from Group Books.

WORSHIP ON A RETREAT

The retreat setting offers wonderful opportunities for

special worship experiences. The intense time together creates a basic community which acts like a huge call to worship. The preparation is built by the fellowship environment. The closing worship celebration is always a powerful moment.

Our retreat was held in a convent which opened its facilities to others. I slept in the guest room used by Mother Teresa a few weeks earlier. The 125 teenagers had focused on discipleship.

We opened our time together with a Friday evening worship. The next day we focused on a Bible study and a plunge into the nearby community. The youth interviewed local people with cassette tape recorders in an attempt to understand the needs of those in the world around us.

At the closing worship service, we focused on the theme of the book of Jonah. Several of the youth built a huge "whale" out of a piece of 100-foot-by-24-foot 4 mil plastic. They created a huge envelope by taping the outside edges together and the open end. A vertical slit was cut in the closed end for the students to enter. A large window fan was taped into the opposite end. We had a moment of crisis when we were beginning to construct the "whale": When the box containing the plastic was opened, we found that it was black! We had expected the transparent material. I didn't know what we would do. We had designed the worship service to take place in the transparent whale. We were gong to show slides of ocean scenes on the sides.

The teenagers came to the rescue. They constructed a huge black whale including a tail. The team solved the light problem by cutting pie-shaped holes in the top of the "whale." These were "blow" holes for the whale to breathe and for us to see.

The call to worship was celebrated by the team bringing each young person into the room and seating him or her on the floor around the uninflated whale. The lights were low.

The worship leader asked the students to focus on the people left behind who needed them. We played two different recordings of the song, "You Got a Friend." The students were asked to share some of the images which came to them as they thought about those in need for our prayers of intercession. One girl said that she was praying for a friend with whom she had a fight. She broke into tears as she told us about his death in a car accident a few days later.

The teenager who was leading the service read selections from the book of Jonah. She then offered a prayer of petition asking God to provide a place of security during our time of need. The fan was switched on. The whale slowly inflated. (There is always an audible expression of amazement when a group first sees the inflated plastic structure.)

We stood, joined hands, sang a song, and wound our way around the room and into the whale. The teenagers sat down once they were all inside. It was dark, but we could see our surroundings.

For the prayer act of confession, the leader told about the fear and uncertainty felt by Jonah when he was in the belly of the giant sea animal. She had the youth focus on their own burden of sin. The darkness helped to create a sense of honesty and sharing. One young woman told us that she needed forgiveness. "A man killed my dad last year. I just can't forgive him." The prayer and love energy of the whole group focused on her. She cried and several people hugged her.

Another voice was heard with words of care and assurance that God would forgive her and give her the capacity to forgive when the time was right.

We sang another song. One of the teenagers carried in the bread and a cup of grape juice. I conducted the words of institution for the Lord's Supper. The teenagers passed the loaf and broke off pieces of it for each other. The cup was passed and the youth dipped the bread in the juice.

The worship team led a prayer of thanksgiving. We gave an offering to each young person—a small washer which is used on bolts and nuts. This was to symbolize the unity of the community of faith as we are apart from one another.

The benediction was a charge to be set forth to do our ministry like Jonah. The young people poured out of the whale with song.

WORSHIP AT A WORKCAMP

The workcamp setting draws young people into a fresh close relationship with the lives of others. They are able to give themselves in Christian service while discovering the incredible gift that only others can give to them. Recognizing the contributions made to one's spiritual life by those being served is a remarkable step to Christian maturity.

The most important vehicle for the communication and celebration of faith is the story. A religious educator suggests that every Christian must have several stories to tell. The first story is the account of creation. After moving through the stories of salvation in the Bible, each of us must be able to tell the story of our faith tradition and finally our own faith experience. The educator concludes that the role of the worship leader or minister is to build a fire around which people can tell their stories.

One group of young people were on a workcamp in the rural area of West Virginia. The worship services took place at night around a campfire. The evening celebrations included local people as well as visiting teenagers. The young people asked an old woman whose house they were rebuilding to play her guitar for them at each service.

Once they had the music for the service, they urged the local people to tell their life stories. Each night they featured a different person. It was amazing how biblical, emotional and challenging these tales were. They were everything a great sermon should be. The students discovered that these people made no separation between their life experiences and their faith.

The prayer time was a community affair. The young worship leader passed around something which had played a role in the day's work as the focus for the prayer concerns. On different evenings he chose a piece of wood, a hammer, a used piece of tar paper (from a repaired roof) and an old family Bible.

The leader passed the item around the campfire and asked each person to share the ways that item revealed a prayer concern (thanksgiving, confession, intercession or petition). For instance, the night they used the wood, some people said it was similar to the imperfections in their own lives. After this process of confession, the wood was thrown into the fire. The group then reflected on how the burning wood affirmed the forgiveness given by God in Jesus Christ. The local people were particularly open in their sharing in this way.

WORSHIP ON THANKSGIVING

The church turned over the Thanksgiving morning service to the leadership of the youth group. The youth had been studying the hunger needs of the world. Their Bible study had confirmed the conviction that as they worked to feed the hungry person, they were serving Jesus.

The young people prepared for the service by gathering two spoons for each person. The teenagers also found a picture of a starving child. Using an electronic stencil maker, they mimeographed the picture for the bulletin cover.

When the congregation entered the church, each worshiper was handed two spoons. The call to worship was led by having the worshipers meditate on the bulletin cover. The young worship leader asked the congregation to study the picture closely to discover why God was calling them to worship on this day.

The prayer of confession followed. Another youth read the scripture passage to call them to confess their sins. The congregation was then asked to look at themselves in the upside-down reflection of their spoons. How can their sins turn their world upside down?

The worship leader then read words of assurance concerning their forgiveness. They were told to turn the spoons to the other side (and the reflection is now right-side-up). The congregation was asked to look at its restored image and accept the fact that they are forgiven. The music for the service was accompanied by the worshipers playing their spoons. This was done by simple instructions from the music director.

The prayer act of intercession for the hungry of the world was undertaken with the use of the spoons. The worshipers were asked to place one of their spoons in their mouth. During this time of prayer, the leader read an account of the hunger situation in Africa. Of course, the taste of an empty spoon makes an incredible impact. The taste of metal where there should be food is surprisingly disturbing.

The prayer act of petition was celebrated by the worship leader asking the congregation to share aloud ways by which spoons meet our needs. For example, to help take medicine, to help prepare and eat food, etc.

The Word focused on Matthew 25:31-46. The passage was read. Several teenagers mimed the opportunity to serve Christ through helping those who are hungry, thirsty, lonely, strangers, naked, sick and in prison.

The minister then served communion. The worshipers passed the bread and partook of it in the pews. They were invited to come forward as the juice was poured into the spoons.

The offering was taken for their local hunger pantry. The parting focused on the spoons. The participants were asked to remember that Jesus told them to remember him as often as they eat and drink. "Each time you look at a spoon remember that God feeds us in order that we may feed others." The spoons were returned to the baskets at the door.

CHRISTMAS WORSHIP: INSIDE AND OUTSIDE

The Christmas season is one of the most dramatic and exciting parts of the church year. The birth of Christ promises hope and new life to every difficult human condition. One of the real gifts of this season is that most churches are prepared for something special in worship.

This youth-organized model for Christmas, draws from the experience of several churches and utilizes a great deal of work. In fact, the youth worship committee begins its work on the service in September. The goal of this service is to reach as many people as possible with the implications of Christ's birth.

There are two levels to this unusual worship service. The first is the public program. The youth build five displays along the driveway and parking lot of the church. These sites are built of wood and can stand the weather for the 10 days they will be used.

The scenes include Mary with the angel of God telling her about the birth of Christ (the call to worship), the shepherds receiving the Good News (prayer of praise), the wisemen (prayer of intercession), the family of Jesus with the newborn Savior (the Gospel) and the faith at work today (commissioning). These Christmas vignettes are staffed by people playing the roles of the biblical characters. Live animals are used in several of them.

A tape is made for each booth. The speakers are directed to face the cars in front of that particular booth. This means that each cluster of cars can hear its tape without being bothered by the others. Each car is given an order of worship. This outlines the "moving" service with scripture passages. Of course, the bulletin invites them to attend Christmas Eve and Christmas Day services.

The cars move along the line of the displays and stop in the area. The tapes are quite short—each run about 60 to 90 seconds. The church has a huge parking area. People are invited to come into the church for hot cider and cornbread. There is a group of teenagers who act as hosts in this area. A surprising number of people remain for this informal time.

The popularity of this unique worship experience has been unbelievable. The cars are lined up for miles! The church has to hire a police officer to direct traffic. The cars are often packed with people. They have developed a special route for the cars to approach the church so that the main road will not be choked with traffic.

The second part of this worship is the Christmas Eve service. The outdoor event creates so much interest that the youth group members have to offer three Christmas Eve services. They take some of the materials from their outside displays for their inside services.

When the youth were planning the Christmas Eve service, they focused on the excitement which particularly grips children at this time of the year. How could they pick up this thrilling state of mind and relate it to the birth of Christ? Clowns, balloons, physical involvement, the birth and the use of light all seemed to be clues to help capture this excitement.

As the families came into the evening services, they were greeted with several colorful clowns. The youth who provide this ministry are trained as theological clowns. They use pantomine and work to welcome everyone to the house of God. A helium-filled balloon was tied to the wrist of every person. Attached to each balloon was a piece of paper which would be used later on in the service.

Other clowns gave out pieces of wood to create music during the service. The young people received these from the local high school shop class. People in the community are glad to donate items when they realize how they will be used.

As the people came into the service, folk carols were being sung. The young song leader encouraged the congregation to use their blocks of wood to create the music. The physical involvement seemed to trigger a spirit of anticipation.

The prayers were offered through skits and mime. The clowns led the congregation through a time of confession and pardon, intercession, petition and thanksgiving.

The Gospel lesson featured the account from Luke 2. While this was read, the couple who had participated in the outside booth came down the aisle with their real baby. The children were invited to gather on the steps around the "holy" family which was sitting in at the front of the church. The sermon was presented as a first-person dialogue from the couple. They told their story as Mary and Joseph. They had a very winning manner which enabled them to work in the questions and comments of the children. This was not a "children's" sermon. It was a homily for the whole people of God. It just happened to be an inclusive experience which touched the young and old alike.

The service was closed by the teenagers carrying in a huge birthday cake with one lighted candle. The congregation played their blocks of wood and sang "Happy Birthday." The worshipers were asked to write a brief Christmas message on a small piece of paper which was attached to their balloons. Then, they were invited to the front for a piece of birthday cake. After they had finished their cake, the congregation went outside and released their balloons. Christmas can be a very special time to release the creative contributions of teenagers in leading and planning congregational worship.

EASTER SUNRISE SERVICE

The Easter sunrise service sponsored by the youth group is one of the wonderful traditions for many churches. It may seem that only teenagers could be foolish enough to get up at such an early hour. I remember those sleepless nights before these 6 a.m. worship experiences as I wondered if I would be able to do my part properly. I still can feel the excitement of leading worship at the crack of dawn. Perhaps I am a minister today because of the church's affirming by giving me worship responsibilities at these sunrise services when I was young.

This biblical story begs that we choose settings and worship approaches to help our youth enter into the wonder of the Resurrection.

If weather permits in your area, go to a garden setting to take the worshipers into John 20:1-18. Or find a cemetery or rocky area to hold the service. It is helpful if several local youth groups can sponsor such a service. The Resurrection celebration is an ideal time to bring Christians together in worship.

We held such a service in an old downtown church. Instead of using the usual worship area, we chose a dark sub-basement. This was a large half-developed space under a regular basement.

We met in the upper basement. The call to worship was drawn right from John 20:1. A teenager came running into the room and cried over and over, "The stone is rolled away! The stone is rolled away! They have taken Jesus away. They have taken him away!"

Several other young people assumed the roles of Peter and the beloved disciple. They told everyone to be totally quiet. It was important that we didn't arouse the guards. (The teenagers were not actors. We did not write script. Please don't disregard this model because it looks so demanding on talent. Your youth are wonderfully outgoing persons. They can easily develop and play the role of biblical people. I am always amazed how this experience of crawling inside a biblical character changes the partici- pants. They really understand how God is working on and through this person in a special way.)

Moving swiftly and quietly, the worship community joined hands and wove their ways along the winding path to the sub-basement. The room was very dimly lighted. Only a small candle flickered near a pile of white cloth. The white clot represented the wrapping around Jesus' head.

The other disciple mentioned in verse 8 was played by a teenager named Tom. He gave a monologue about his doubt and sin (the prayer act of confession). Tom passed the white cloth from person to person and asked the wor- shipers to share by saying, "Lord, when I fail, help me _____."

The worship leader went to each person and placed the napkin on his or her head and said, "Brother/Sister, the Lord Jesus was raised from the dead so that your sins may be forgiven."

The young woman playing the role of Mary Magdalene came rushing in and told her story about meeting Jesus in the garden.

She ended her sharing with the question, "How am I going to make the others believe what I have seen and heard?" The next few minutes became a dialogue with the worshipers. What makes it so hard to believe in Jesus in our time?

During the offering, each young person was given a "Resurrection" stone that we had gathered outside the church.

The parting charge was to "tell others about what we have seen" (verse 18). We hummed all of the Easter hymns during this service. We were amazed by the power of this simple way of communicating the message of the great Easter hymns.

We always try to have a breakfast time after this Sun- rise service. It fits in with the several post-Resurrection meals Jesus had with his disciples.

ALL SAINTS DAY

This worship event is one of the most amazing and successful intergenerational celebrations I have experienced. Ed McNulty is responsible for this special worship. He got his inspiration from Harvey Cox's exposition on the feast in the Middle Ages where the world was turned upside down and people became fools for Christ.

Everyone in the church and community was invited. They were encouraged to wear a costume of a medieval person whose place they would like to take. The worship celebration was held the Sunday of or before All Saints Day. This comes at the beginning of November or the end of October. This celebration was developed in the early days of the church. The first reference is found in A.D. 373.

Ed uses the largest possible space and transforms it to a medieval festival. The idea is to keep everything and everyone together yet free to wander from activity to activity. This worship experience is designed to permit the young and old to become a child again in the community of saints. There is fun, festivity and Christian celebration in this delightful time.

The service ran from 5:30 p.m. to 8 p.m., allowing plenty of time for cleanup and for children and older people to get home early. A medieval theme was stressed in decorations—lots of banners on the walls and streaming flags. One of the young people did a great job playing the role of the court jester. He was costumed for the part and served as the host. He drew attention to the activities and made people feel at home with humor and warmth.

Other parish families helped set up and serve simple meals such as chicken, cheese, vegetables and bread. The food was served in bowls and people had to eat with their hands.

The schedule followed this pattern. Hosts greeted people with great love and excitement for the call to worship. They were given simple costume items if they did not come in special garb. A small cross was drawn on their cheek as a sign of their acceptance into the family of faith.

The first half-hour was spent looking at one another. There was a wild assortment of medieval pages, knights,

Robin Hoods, Maid Marians, monks, nuns, princesses, tramps, etc.

The community gathered at the long tables for prayers of intercession for those who had nothing to eat. They then ate with their fingers in the style of the times. As the people finished their food, the following nine interest centers opened: banner making, a graffiti wall, mask construction, the building of an 8-foot cross out of boxes and news pictures, a frame for a huge George and the Dragon, crafts, apple bobbing, a humorous skit on the inquisition, and a haunted dungeon.

Toward the close of the evening, the community gathered around the 8-foot cross. The people sang the theme song, "Lord of the Dance," by Sydney Carter. The participants moved in long lines as they sang it over and over.

Then people went to the cross and found a picture or caption in the collage. They offered a prayer about a need triggered by the story or picture.

The Word came in the presentation of the skit about the inquisition. Then the youth presented a short slide-and-sound show featuring the saints who made the feast possible: Adam and Eve, Abraham and Sarah, Moses, Joshua, Isaiah, Jesus, Peter, Paul, Calvin, Luther, Pope John, Martin Luther King, Mother Teresa, etc.

As the offering, people shared what they had created in the interest centers. This included all kinds of wonderful banners and collages made by the young and the old. It was a wonderful time for all the saints, living and dead.

LENTEN SERIES

This series of six services was planned by youth, but received a lot of help from ministers and other adults. The church felt that the pre-Easter season was an important time to reach out to the inactives in the community.

The team presented six radically different worship experiences as a positive event in the life of the congregation. Often alternative worship ideas presented by youth meet with surprise and even criticism. This team avoided this problem by doing three important things:

1. They warned people that the Sunday morning events would be different from the past. This meant that people who had a determined contract on what worship would be would not feel that they had been betrayed.

2. They built a carefully explained and well-advertised rationale for these six unusual worship events. People invited friends to this very special series.

3. They involved youth in the planning and execution of the worship. This partnership gave the ministers a reason for change and the resource of super ideas and energy.

PART ONE

The Jewish Service—300 B.C.

This service was developed with the help of the local rabbi. Both ministers had taken Hebrew in seminary and were able to handle some of the prayers in that language.

When the people gathered in the narthex, they were called to worship by the ancient tradition of blowing a ram's horn. Small hats were given to each person. The women were seated on one side of the sanctuary; the men were seated on the other. The bulletin was totally changed in format. The back page gave a clear and concise rationale for this particular service as part of our history. (All bulletins in each of the six services must contain the history of the period you are celebrating.)

The clergy and assistants were dressed in ancient robes. These had been borrowed from the local Masonic lodge. The congregation even used Jewish prayer books (with English translations). For music they used the flute key on the organ, plus two flutists. They wanted to use a cantor, but were unable to get one for the service.

The sermon was the dramatic scene from Jeremiah 18:1-12. The young people asked a potter in the community to show the minister how to work a bit at the wheel. The message of judgment featured the breaking of a pot on the floor of the sanctuary. The minister was quite frightened to try this unusual presentation. It was the teenagers who supported, aided and encouraged him to make this leap to a dramatic form.

The pieces from the pot were distributed to the congregation. They were asked to reflect on them as they came before God with their prayers of confession and intercession.

At the benediction, the participants were asked to put the piece of the broken pot in their wallet, pocket or purse and carry it for the next week as a sign of their responsibility to be faithful to their convenant with God.

This service also provided the benefit of establishing a relationship between the local rabbi and the church's ministers. Further exchanges developed between the youth groups.

PART TWO
The Catacombs—A.D. 200

This service was held in the fellowship hall of the church, because it had more space than the sanctuary. Teenagers greeted the worshipers at the main doors and used felt markers to draw a small fish (two curved lives intersecting each other) on the back of the people's hands.

The youth had placed the fish emblem every few feet along the wall to direct the participants to the worship area. The worshipers were warned that it was dangerous and that everyone should be very quiet.

The room was very dark with a candle providing the only light.

Youth group members greeted each person, looked for his or her sign of being Christ's follower (the fish), and led the worshiper by the hand to his or her seat.

The clergy and youth leaders were dressed in period costumes which they had borrowed from the community and high school drama groups and the Masonic lodge.

The music was provided by recorders. These instruments are later than this period; however, the recorders gave the service a personal feeling. The service was very simple yet instructional. People sang Psalms, prayed and listened to a meditation from the Sermon on the Mount. The leaders took turns presenting the meditation teachings as if they were providing guidelines for the worshipers who were living in a non-Christian world.

The prayers were presented as if a letter had been written by a preacher who was not present (similar to Paul's letters to the Corinthians). It mentioned the need to support other Christians. The offering came after this.

Near the end of the service, the leaders kept telling the people to be quiet; they might be overheard. Two policemen barged into the service and announced that everyone was arrested. (This had been arranged previously with two officers.) It was just real enough to stun the congregation. The pastors agreed to go in place of the people; they were led out. At the door, one pastor stopped and gave the benediction. The doors closed and the service was over. Coffee was served.

The discussion after the service was fantastic. The young people served as hosts. One teenager asked the people to share the moments which touched them the most during the service. A couple of people said that they wanted to leave the sign of the fish on their hands until next week. What would people say when they saw it?

PART THREE
Reformation Service—A.D. 1542

If you are a Catholic reader, please don't be put off by this title. While this model was developed by a protestant church, you can just as easily develop a scripture service using some of the rich Catholic liturgical heritage from the same period of time.

The attendance kept climbing during the series; people are very enthused about special services. The bulletin must always carry the history behind each of the practices used in the service.

The team looked back in liturgical history to find the actual services used during this period of time. There seemed to be many written prayers and responses, so this was the format which was used. The worship leaders dressed in the black academic gowns and collars of the time.

No instrumental music was used. Only Psalms were sung. (Another reformed tradition might choose different music.) Crosses, banners and some of the windows in the church were covered, following the pattern of Calvin and others who resisted many of the art forms found in the churches of the day.

The sermon was very strict and long; it dealt with covenant and our responsibility. The worshipers spent a lengthy time on confession and preparation for the Lord's Supper. Communion was then celebrated. The people came forward and knelt. (This was not the custom of the local church.)

The worshipers were sent out in the world to work hard and fulfill the destiny which God had ordained. This service was similar to the usual worship experiences of the church. The planning team wanted to stabilize the series by having a middle worship service which gave the people a chance to get their bearings.

PART FOUR

The Colonial Service—A.D. 1752

The planning team found a great deal of material from this period by looking through the records from the local historical societies. The service featured the clothes from the period. The order of worship was quite similar to what the congregation had been using.

The unusual aspect of the service was the use of communion tokens. These small pieces of leather, lead and wood were given by the church elders to people who were prepared to receive the Lord's Supper. No one could take the sacrament without a token. (This was a law in many parts of the colonies.)

In the late 1700's, the elders would visit all members and check to see if they were living in reconciliation with their brothers and sisters. The elders were judges, marriage counselors and law enforcement agents.

You could use this feature of the service for a calling program for every member of the church. Certain members could wear tricorn hats and call on others. After prayer and conversation, each person could be given a token. The church may no longer use this screening process; however, preparation for communion always is proper.

This congregation made tokens from pieces of scrap metal which had been created by stamping holes in a tool plant owned by a relative of a member. They had a simple die made and the slugs were stamped with the date and name of the church. The tokens cost very little; yet they became a treasured token for those who attended the worship.

When the time for communion came, the people came forth and presented their token. After the Lord's Supper, the pastor announced that members had been at the table of God. The teenagers redistributed the tokens to the worshipers and said, "Carry the token as a symbol to remind you that you have been to the table."

PART FIVE
The Wild West—A.D. 1880

If the weather permits, this is the perfect service for the parking lot, nearby park or church lawn. This service is the frontier revival format. The local western store loaned the worship leaders hats and coats. The ushers and choir members also were dressed in this style.

A song leader led old Gospel hymns. The choir sat out in the congregation.

Informality was the order of the day. They tried to recapture the excitement of the worship service among people who did not often have the opportunity to meet. The visit of a guest preacher was a special occasion.

Before the service, a few people were alerted that the opportunity would be given for prayers. These people responded when the time came for the different prayers. Others quickly joined in.

The sermon was a revival style with the focus on "hell and brimstone." It was not a joke or takeoff on such a message; in fact, the sermon ended with an altar call. A number of people came forward and rededicated their lives. This was not a usual part of the service; it was a very moving worship experience.

PART SIX
Futuristic Service—A.D. 2001

This was the wildest and the most exciting service in the series. The young people prepared the fellowship hall in a most unusual manner. They obtained two huge sheets of 4 mil plastic. They taped it together with transparent freezer tape on both sides along the center seam. This made a 100-foot-by-32-foot sheet.

The edges of the plastic were taped to the floor. Two large window fans were taped into one end of the plastic. The other end was taped down and a slit was cut in the middle to provide a doorway. When the fans were turned on, the plastic became a huge inflated structure. Within this "plastic spaceship," chairs were arranged in three rows on each side facing each other.

Several large weather balloons were inflated and fastened to the ceiling. Slide projectors were positioned to show slides of planets on the balloons. These images give the striking impression of being actual planets.

The teenagers dressed in jackets and acted as space stewards. They checked people in for the space flight. They gave them boarding passes with their names on them.

The room was darkened. The people were led to the rows of chairs within the plastic spaceship.

The "captain" welcomed the people aboard for the space journey. "We will be worshiping in shallow space today. As we lift off you may notice some change in sound, but there should be little other change in our environment."

A tape was played which contained a countdown from a space shuttle flight. As the sound faded, the slide projectors were turned on and the worshipers could see the "planets" in the sky. The view through the plastic made the planets look real.

We then used the usual Lutheran liturgy as our order of worship. However, we had changed each item into a "spacelike" language. For example, "The Lord be with you space travellers."

"And also with you, Captain."

The music was on tape. We were able to get some popular hymns played on electronic instruments. It provided a most unusual background for our singing.

Everyone was given a "moon" rock. This became the focus for the prayers. The worship leader read statements about the nature of the world at this time (2001). These projections were gathered from a couple of the popular futuristic books. For instance, the prayer act of confession was undertaken by asking each person to feel his or her moon rock and offer a prayer item concerning the time when there are no more fish in the seas because of pollution.

The love feast was served in small plastic cups and the bread was a rationlike substance. The pastor focused on the continuity between the ancient past and the distant future. The communion table spans all time and gives us a sense of the eternal promise. We will not be deserted.

The group returned to earth with the benediction. Everyone was invited to a coffee hour where they would pick up the themes of the future for further discussion and possible action in the four areas of: unemployment, hunger, pollution and change in the family structure.

The planners were delighted by how many people stayed for this act of commitment following the service. This was an extremely popular series. The team found that the congregation was much more open to the changes youth wanted after going through this series. The leaders felt that the church had a better understanding of worship after experiencing these different formats.

CHAPTER 17

A Workshop Model for Creative Worship

The 800 youth leaped from their seats and scattered in every direction. The sound level in the room seemed to explode. Fifty teenagers at the back of the huge hall clawed their way through a large pile of junk. Excitement and confusion echoed through the college gym. These people were scrambling to a worship service which would take place in 20 minutes. No one was directing them; they were undertaking this important task on their own.

This scene represents one of the most exciting aspects of my work with youth. These young people were participating in a workshop to train them how to design *their own* authentic worship experiences.

There is always a danger that some people will misunderstand the term ''youth worship.'' This book has attempted to show that ''youth worship'' does not denote anything mysterious. We have looked at simple ways to create worship experiences that touch young people in special ways. Granted, there is in a sense only one kind of Christian celebration—authentic worship that glorifies God. Perhaps it is more accurate to talk about ''worship *by* youth'' rather than ''worship *for* youth.''

All the ideas in this book focus on drawing young people into a worshipful relationship with God and the community of faith. It is certainly possible to have this relationship in the context of traditional forms. However, the amazing variety of worship styles throughout the world and over the centuries suggests that God nurtures countless ways to worship him. Indeed, one can make a case that there are as many ways to worship God as there are Christians.

It's helpful to realize that God became flesh in order to involve us more deeply in the gift of salvation. The Lord reached out to us in the most creative way possible so that we would know the truth most intimately and immediately. Those who plan and lead worship have the basic task to create meaningful experiences that help people understand and glorify God with intimacy and immediacy. This is an awesome challenge regardless of the age of the people or the setting.

Young people have most clearly revealed their creative and spiritual resources to me when I have turned over the task of worship design and leadership to them. I have led many such events with every age group in a number of different cultures. I have also had good experience with intergenerational worship gatherings.

I don't believe that we should "dump" the sensitive responsibility of worship leadership onto the laps of people who don't know what to do. The worship of God is too serious to be casually undertaken. Yet, with the supportive context of the Christian community, the presence of the Holy Spirit, and a clear focus, young believers do have incredible resources which are untapped. The following workshop model will help you tap the resources for creative worship within young people. I've used it for years in a variety of settings. I trust that it will assist you in your setting.

A SIMPLE WORSHIP MODEL

THE LEADER

The key to worthy worship experiences among youth

is, of course, leadership. The way the leader sets the pace for the process is extremely important. I enter such experiences with a very positive outlook. I believe that God will work through the young people who will plan worship. We tend to receive from people what we expect from them. If you are cynical and suspicious of young people, they won't fail to live *down* to your expectations in worship planning.

Young people have ministered to me in so many ways. My whole life is a living testimony that God speaks through young people. My radio and television work in the past 20 years have been a constant partnership with teenagers. God works through the young in a very special way.

Young people live to gain experience and wisdom; yet, they already have experience and wisdom. Most of them have sat through hundreds of worship services. They have been bathed in the love of the Christian community for years.

The young also have very special emotional entry points to the story of salvation because of their weaknesses and needs. One of the abiding themes of scripture is that the Messianic message comes through the vulnerability of the servant. For the Christian, weakness is a spiritual strength.

Young people also have amazing energy and restlessness. What wonderful gifts for the faith community! The slumbering faith community so desperately needs energy and restlessness. The worship of God cries out for vitality and curiosity. The young are often barometers for the unexpressed attitudes of the adult community. "The fathers have eaten sour grapes, and the children's teeth are set on edge" (Jeremiah 31:29). A teenager may skip worship because it is boring, while the equally bored adult sleeps through the service. Aren't they both making the same judgment about what is or is not happening in worship?

THE SETTING

Let's work through a typical event. I usually prefer to conduct the worship workshop in the context of a whole day. The youth event may have a theme such as, "God so loved the world ..." Let's say that there are 200 young people attending this Saturday event. These youth come

from a number of churches. They may have come from a
large geographical area.

THE OPENING

I like to begin with "a ball of energy" which will set
the tone for the time together. It is imperative that the
leader does not ask the participants to do anything which
they are not willing to do. For example, I begin a workshop with a dramatic opening which indicates that I will
risk.

For instance, one opening is my "Star Wars" event.
The room is darkened. The music from the movie is
played. A slide which announces "Star Wars" is flashed
on the screen. I come running from the back of the room
with my famous Ben Kenobi robe covering my head and
body. I wave my light sabre (flashlight with long white
plastic tube extending about three feet) over the heads of
the young people. I then tell the participants the story of
one of the "Star Wars" films as slides from the movie are
shown on the screen.

Next, I ask for the lights and talk about how God is
Lord over all the cosmos. On one level we must take the
popular culture (e.g., "Star Wars") and use it to glorify
God. But we should not let other people create for us. Our
own imaginations are a gift of God and must be used.

SPACE COMMUNITIES

You can use the same type of opening, then urge the
students to form "space communities" by having one person find another who has the same color of eyes or some
other random similarity. After each person has found
another and sat down, encourage the youth to talk about
some aspect of the theme. Then urge the dyads to find
another pair. After more sharing, this process continues
until you have groups of 16 or so.

Next, have the students close their eyes and imagine
that they are on their way to another planet. All they have
as a community is a common faith as expressed in John
3:16. It is their task as a space community to accomplish
four goals in the next few minutes: Name their new com-

munity; establish how they are going to be ruled in their world; create a way that the wealth will be distributed in their world; and create a one-minute message from their world (based on John 3:16) to our gathering. Everyone in the group should be in the presentation.

Point to a huge pile of "space waste" and tell the students to use this material to create the characterizations for their skit. "Space waste" can consist of cloth scraps, toys, tools, clothing, newspapers, etc. Tell the students to use their creativity and imagination. In this biblical exercise, anything they can imagine can become reality in their new world. (In my opening appearance, I modeled the kind of imagination I asked the students to undertake.) In other words, if the leader will put on a brown robe and wave a child's toy, the students can do the same or better.

Wander among the groups (in your space garb) and check on how things are going. I have noticed a pattern in this workshop model. There is usually a sense of confusion during the first few minutes. I have not chosen any leaders. They look at the sheet that summarizes my oral instructions. My visits just nudge and encourage. Leadership seems to emerge. Some groups go to the pile of waste and get their ideas from the objects. They always develop the ideas to share in the last five or six minutes before we are scheduled to meet.

Call together the total community and have the space groups share the messages from their world. One group of young people clapped pieces of wood together as they walked to the center of the room. One young person dressed as an extraterrestrial by wrapping himself like a mummy and using two potato scrub brushes as ears. The spokesman said, "When people on our planet get caught up in hatred, we have a way of forgiving them." He then took a pan of water and sprinkled the extraterrestrial and the rest of the worshipers.

As of this writing, I have led this segment with about 100 different youth gatherings all over the world. The youth are always fantastic. We laugh, applaud and have moments of tears in this time of sharing. No event is ever the same.

TALKING TO ALIENS

At the end of this celebration declare that the people on earth are not aliens. How can we bring the Good News of John 3:16 to this strange people? We first must learn who they are.

Take the participants through a brief orientation concerning their plunge into the community. They will go out as space communities into the immediate area for the next 90 minutes. These earthlings will not know that they are from another planet.

Prior to the worship, ask the youth to bring their tape recorders. At least one recorder is needed for every five or six teenagers.

The students' task is to interview strangers in the community. Show them how to listen to the stories of these people. I have developed a three-step approach for interviews:

1. The contract. Establish trust with the person being interviewed by saying who you are, what you are doing and why you are interviewing.

2. The encounter. Use questions that don't have a wrong answer; for example, "If you had five minutes to live, how would you spend this time?" "With whom would you spend this time?" "Why?"

3. The conclusion. Say thank you and affirm the interviewees' act of sharing themselves with others.

Run through this process of interviewing with examples from such encounters of others. Depending on the time, pair the participants and have them use spoons as substitutes for microphones to take turns interviewing each other.

Ask the groups to accomplish the following tasks during the next 90 minutes: Every person or pair within a space community should get an interview; find lunch somewhere along the way; and stay together as a group when you are out in the world. Discover the needs and strengths of these strange humans. Listening is the most important part of good interviewing.

Offer to clean and check the participants' tape recorders before they leave. This is done with isopropyl alcohol and cotton tips. Always have spare batteries and extra tapes.

Dismiss the students for their plunge into this alien world. There is always a mixture of fear and excitement. A couple groups will need words of assurance and clarification.

DEBRIEFING

It is always exciting to see the teenagers and adults return from such a plunge. Many are in a daze from the kinds of experiences they have had. Others are bubbling with excitement about the experience. Most are deeply touched by the people they have met.

Young people have a special way of relating to others. For example, a pair of students interviewed two street people in Boston. The students were able to get meaningful and moving stories from these special people. Strangers often tell these young people things which they have never told anyone else.

We can spend as much time as we want on this process. Every student has a story. I usually don't ask them to play their interviews for the whole group; it takes too much time. The group begins to discover the needs and gifts of these strangers. Keep asking the students how we should approach such people with the Gospel.

PREPARING FOR THE WORSHIP WORKSHOP

After this sharing, assign each group a portion of the worship service which they will lead in the late afternoon. Use the basic structure described in this book: call to worship, invocation, prayer of thanksgiving, prayers of confession and pardon, prayer of intercession, prayer of petition, music group, the Word—Old Testament, the Word—New Testament, the offering, the love feast, the parting. Pass out a sheet to each group with their portion of the service marked. Have several tables staffed with skilled people in areas such as dance, music, simple media, etc. Tell the groups to seek any special skills they need.

Give brief summaries of each section of the service. After each part, remind the youth to utilize any way which will help us become involved in this aspect of worshiping God. It is important to repeat the charge to create new forms.

Most of the sections are self-explanatory. However, the sections on the Word are usually presented as if they are the sermon portion of the service. Assign particular passages to the groups that are assigned these sections. Visit these groups and encourage them to use mime or some other non-preaching approach. The young people always jump right into the idea.

Give the music group license to bring in songs at any point in the service. They may go to the music resource table for special help. They may even raid other groups for musicians.

The love feast is sometimes an actual snack time. You could choose "healthy" foods such as nuts and fruits. Other times, the love feast is much closer to a communion service. This all depends on the tradition of the group.

LET THE SPIRIT LEAD THROUGH THE YOUNG PEOPLE

You will need varying amounts of time to enjoy this worship service. Depending on the number of participants, this service could last from one to two hours. Since the worship is at the end of the workshop experience, be sure to notify parents, bus drivers or camp personnel as to your approximate finishing time.

When the students have convened for the worship experience, post the order of worship and announce, "Let us worship God." It is important to step aside and leave everything in the hands of the teenagers. There will be times when you will feel the need to intrude and get things moving or change the direction of the service. However, it is vital that you don't do anything.

I remember one super event in California. The 500 students were conducting a fantastic service of their own design. We were moving to a peak experience when the teenagers in charge of the next section asked us to arise and go outside. I felt that this was the wrong thing to do. We were building for a spiritual point which would be upset by such a break. Yet, I was committed to let God work through these young people.

We went outside and formed two long lines facing each other. There was a sense of play as we made our prayer act of confession by playing "Red Rover, Red Rover, Send (Name) Right Over." People would then rush across the field and try to break into the other line. There was rejection and anger when a person broke the line or failed to get through the web of linked hands.

After a few minutes of furious competition and separation, the team of young people led us through some exercises of forgiveness and reconciliation. We were soon a circle of believers again. When we entered the hall for the remainder of the service; we were ready for a peak exercise. The Spirit was leading the teenagers to do the proper thing. Thank God I stayed quiet and let them lead us.

Many of the worship ideas in this book have been developed by young people in this kind of workshop worship. I love this model. If things don't work out, the participants can say that Benson was a lousy leader. If it goes very well, the young people can go home knowing that they did a good job.

The discomfort in this kind of design for the leadership is that you must put your trust into the hands of the teenagers. When young people suddenly realize that they are in control, they rise to the challenge. One young person told me how his life was changed in the course of such a service. "I have never been in front of 1,400 people before. When I started doing my part in the mime presentation of the Word, I could feel all those people pulling for me. It felt as if God was coming into my life like never before."

I remember a time in Oregon when we were deeply involved in the confession in the youth service. A young woman played a segment of her interview with a man she had found on his hands and knees on the sidewalk. He was trying to spit and fill the crack in the concrete. She got down on the sidewalk and interviewed this lost soul. He talked about his former home and family. The young woman played a 60-second excerpt and asked us to pray for him. Out of the darkness another strong voice said: "Pray for me. I passed the man and thought he was just a bum."

Sometimes youth have written hymns during the planning time for us to use. At other times, people have created a rhythm band from the whole congregation by passing out pieces of wood and other improvised instruments.

There have been many tears and lots of hugs as these worship experiences end. I remember standing in a small Australian church for an hour after the service. I had given the final benediction after the celebration designed by the group of 50 youth. I told them that this was my last stop on my 12-week Australian trek. When I reminded the youth that we would never be together again in this configuration until we meet in the kingdom of God, I broke down. These young people were not as open in their public expression of emotion; yet, the Spirit of God hung heavily on our hearts. No one wanted to leave.

I remember a group of toughs from inner-city Philadelphia who jumped into this worship model with such energy that a fist fight almost broke out before the service. At the end, five of the teenagers wanted to walk with me as I went to the place where I would be staying. (They felt I needed protection.) The same teenagers were waiting for me the next day to escort me to my preaching engagement. They knew how much I appreciated and respected them.

At another workshop, a young person approached me after I had made the assignments. He was a very nervous young man; he couldn't believe that I was turning the love feast over to the teenagers. "I can't permit myself to be served at the hands of people who don't know the Lord very deeply," he said. I told him that I understood his concern. If he found that this part of the service was handled with any disrespect, he should feel comfortable not participating. However, I urged him to keep an open mind.

The young man came up to me after the service and told me that he had participated and had been deeply touched. It is sometimes difficult for young people to believe in themselves. Yet, I can't repeat too often the basic theme underlying this workshop: God works through teenagers in worship.

Epilogue

I read a recent survey which indicated that teenagers rank the dislike of attending religious services above the dislike of drinking alcohol. Unfortunately, the traditional setting of worship has a bad reputation among many Christian young people. Perhaps young people absorb this attitude from the many bored, sleeping and disinterested adults around them on a Sunday morning. This does not have to be the case. Young people can absorb the wonderful mystery that the Holy Spirit is present in worship and the voice of God is heard in the human heart. Worship is God's feast and we are the people of the Lord.

Our task, as youth leaders, is to help make worship experiences all that they can be: exciting, inspiring, challenging, thought-provoking. Our task also is to enable youth to help plan and participate in creative, meaningful worship experiences.

There are no shortcuts to authentic worship. The finest traditional literary forms, classical music, majestic preaching or dramatic presentations cannot ensure the presence of God. We are the people of God who come before the Word at the beckoning of the Spirit.

The Holy Spirit is the author of the authentic worship; the Spirit is actively working among the community of faith. The Word becomes flesh at these moments of mystery and wonder. Worship events enable people to freely offer the fruit of God working in their lives.

Such freedom actually places a greater burden on the

worship leadership. Our task is to provide the cradle in which this child may be gently nurtured. In other words, our task is to provide the framework in which people can express the gifts God was given them. I trust that you have noted that this book affirms the belief that true authentic freedom in worship can be celebrated only when planning and structure have been provided. It costs to set people free.

I also pray that you have gleaned from these pages that I believe God alone is the Lord of the worship moment. No bag of tricks or gimmicks will displace this center of reality. Only God can bless our efforts at opening the experience of the Word before the people of faith.

In the course of this book, we have seen the work of many brothers and sisters who have risked to be faithful in wondrous and imaginative forms. I remember talking with a favorite church musician. I asked him how he could continue risking in search of fresh modes of worship. He slowly patted his guitar. "I can only give the Lord the very best that I have. This is my very best."

God in no way restricts our imagination. The power of the Word keeps drawing us out of ourselves and into the whole act of worshiping with all of our being. Every fibre of intellect, the fullness of each sense, the boundless depths of imagination and the humblest faults and failures are called into service as we praise the name of the Lord.

I fully understand our temptation to let our needs of self-protection screen out the beckoning paths of creative worship. It *is* easier to repeat the simple formula of last week's and last year's opening worship service for the Sunday evening youth group. Creativity is always difficult and scary work. This book has shown you that the fresh and new are not the elitist possessions of a select few. The inspiration for creative worship is a gift of God which is a blessing for *everyone* in the faith family.

This book exists because of many kindred spirits who have nudged, challenged and supported my probes into worship. Teachers have drummed the history and theology of God's people at worship in many cultures and eras.

It is obvious that many people contributed to the ideas and stories shared in this book. Many ideas will seem

familiar and yet a bit different. As I have stated before:
There are no new ideas. Somewhere, at sometime, someone
has worshiped God by using the idea which you just "in-
vented." I share this not to discourage or trivialize what
you have done. Rather I share this so that we can rejoice in
the realization that creative worship rests in the continuity
of past, present and future. Extend this journey of borrow-
ing and adapting as you reshape what has been shared on
these pages. I thank God for those who have built the
foundation for my ideas and I praise God for you who will
carry on.

I hope that you have found our journey together to be a
complex and stimulating experience. In many ways, this is
a dangerous book. It challenges and pushes all of us to
risk. There will be moments when things will not work
out. You may plan, pray and risk only to have the experience misunderstood.

I have found that God has blessed me most consistently
when I have failed. There is something so wonderful in the
act of throwing ourselves on the mercy of God. "Lord God,
I have failed. Forgive me if I have failed to lead your people to the act of worshiping you. Thank you for leading to
the moment in which I may risk all for you." Feeling
bathed in the cleansing power of God's love is one of God's
greatest gifts.

I wish that I could be with you personally as you pursue authentic and creative worship with the young people
in your life. I know that God will lead you and your youth
as you provide just the right mixture of the traditional and
the unexpected in your worship experiences.

There is an exciting and wonderful journey before you.
May God continue to lead you in this quest. Let us begin.

Creative Youth Ministry Resources for You

Fast Forms for Youth Ministry
compiled by Lee Sparks

Here's a lifesaver for busy youth workers. **Fast Forms for Youth Ministry** gives you more than 80 handy, time-saving forms. You'll save energy and effort. You'll be better organized. Plus, you'll be an even more effective ministry manager.

In just minutes, you can have great-looking forms. Copy and use them directly or use them as models for your own professional-looking . . .

Certificates	Expense sheets
Schedules	Surveys
Awards	Evaluations
Job descriptions	Permission forms

You'll reduce paperwork. Improve communications. And, you'll save hours of work with this practical, time-saving tool.

ISBN 0931-529-25-5, $11.95

Youth Ministry Cargo
by Joani Schultz and dozens of contributors

Get on board for a journey through the kaleidoscope of creative ideas in **Youth Ministry Cargo. Cargo's** packing list includes a variety of topics for meeting young people's needs. You'll be amazed at how simple, everyday objects will help kids grow in their faith. Each entry is followed by "Variations," or alternatives, to help you adapt the idea to meet your group's specific needs. Your group members will enjoy the clever and unique learning approaches. Use these ideas to teach about poverty, self-image, peace and justice issues, Christlike faith, music, worship, and a host of other subjects. Games, craft activities, service projects and fund raisers are also included. Each idea is quick to read and easy to implement. Who knows where your journey will take you as you mix, match, or come up with your own ideas?

ISBN 0931-529-14-X, $18.95

More . . . Group Retreats
edited by Cindy S. Hansen

Bring your group closer together with proven retreats that focus on teenage issues. Choose from 30 carefully designed, ready-to-use retreats covering . . .

- Faith and Commitment
- Stages of Life
- Self-Image
- School—plus 25 other important topics

Each retreat includes step-by-step instructions from start to finish. You'll get detailed time schedules, faith-building activities, inspiring devotional ideas and more. Discover new opportunities for spiritual growth with **More . . . Group Retreats**.

ISBN 0931-529-12-3, $14.95

Improve Your Youth Ministry
With Group Books

Group's Retreat in a Box™: All Stressed Out
by Joani Schultz with Stephen Parolini

Make retreat planning simple! Now you can run a top-notch, meaningful retreat without the usual planning hassles.

Group's Retreat in a Box™: All Stressd Out will help young people conquer the pressures they face at school, home and with friends. Kids will love the special games and zany activities that teach how to . . .
- Cope creatively with stress
- Recognize common pressures
- Slow down and relax
- Discover strength in their faith
- Find support in each other

Now you can enjoy your retreat time too, because everything you need for a fun-filled, faith-building weekend is in the box—including . . .
- ▶ Eye-catching publicity—posters, clip art and announcements
- ▶ Step-by-step leaders guide and easy-to-follow planning guide
- ▶ Flexible scheduling options for groups of 5 - 45
- ▶ Fun games and wacky activities to delight and involve kids
- ▶ Ready-to-copy handouts
- ▶ Audio-tapes—with music, interviews, thought-provoking stories and Bible studies
- ▶ Guided worship experiences and more

Everything about this retreat planner is special. And it's all included. You supply only pencils, Bibles, tape player—and kids!

ISBN 0931-529-38-7, $59.95

Instant Programs for Youth Groups 1, 2, 3
from the editors of Group Publishing

Get loads of quick-and-easy program ideas you can prepare in a flash.

Each meeting idea gives you everything you need for a dynamic program. Step-by-step instructions. Lists of easy-to-find materials. Dynamic discussion starters. And ready-to-copy handouts to involve kids.

Each book gives you 17 (or more) meeting ideas on topics that matter to teenagers . . .
  1—Self-Image, Pressures, Living as a Christian
  2—Me and God, Responsibility, Emotions
  3—Friends, Parents, Dating and Sex

With all three books, you can keep a year's worth of program ideas at your fingertips—ready to tap instantly.

Instant Programs for Youth Groups 1, ISBN 0931-529-32-8, $7.95
Instant Programs for Youth Groups 2, ISBN 0931-529-42-5, $7.95
Instant Programs for Youth Groups 3, ISBN 0931-529-43-3, $7.95

Dynamic Resources for Your Youth Ministry

Parenting Teenagers
Video kit

Offer parents needed support for coping with their teenagers—through practical video training.

Parents will love the insights and encouragement they get from **Parenting Teenagers**. Offer parents in your church practical communication tips, the whys of rebellion, insights into mood swings, ideas for handling peer pressure . . . plus parenting styles, kids' friends and more. Use **Parenting Teenagers** for years to come in parents' meetings, retreats, Sunday school or even by sending videos home with parents!

Your complete kit includes four 30-minute VHS videos and 144-page information-packed leaders guide full of helpful, ready-to-copy worksheets. Discover . . .

Video 1: What Makes Your Teenager Tick?
Video 2: Parenting: How Do You Rate?
Video 3: Communicating With Your Teenager
Video 4: Your Teenager's Friends and Peer Pressure

Give parents of teenagers the support they need to survive the tough teenage years.

ISBN 0931-529-60-3, $98

Training Teenagers for Peer Ministry
by Dr. Barbara B. Varenhorst with Lee Sparks

Expand your ministry effectiveness. Teach your young people how to be skillful care-givers. Use this step-by-step program to enable kids to minister effectively to their friends. The easy-to-follow, activity-rich format equips young people with important life skills . . .

● Making responsible decisons
● Effective listening
● Respecting confidences
● Knowing how to deal with typical teenage concerns, such as family problems, sexual concerns, death and dying

Teach your young people how to turn their faith into real caring, by training your teenagers for peer ministry.

ISBN 0931-529-23-9, $8.95